Make Your Own
TV DINNERS

CAROLINE STEVENS ● DEBORAH ROBB

BOXTREE LTD

This book is dedicated to our husbands, Tom and Hector, who have gamely eaten their way through the contents of this book and have given us their encouragement and support.

First published in 1989 by Boxtree Limited.
In association with Independent Television Productions Ltd

Text © Caroline Stevens & Deborah Robb 1989
Illustrations © Boxtree Limited 1989

Illustrated by Jill Raphaeline
Designed by Bet Ayer
Edited by Jenni Fleetwood
Typeset by Cambrian Typesetters
Printed in Great Britain by
Richard Clay Ltd, Bungay, Suffolk

for Boxtree Limited
36 Tavistock Street
London, WC2E 7PB

British Library Cataloguing in Publication Data
Stevens, Caroline
    Make your own TV dinners.
    1. Food: Time-saving dishes – Recipes
    I. Title   II. Robb, Deborah
    641.5'55

    ISBN 1–85283–263–0

CONTENTS

INTRODUCTION

*I*n today's stressful world, what better way to relax after a hard day than with a delicious meal and a good television programme. All the cares of the day disappear as you escape to foreign lands or mingle with the stars in exotic locations.

This book is designed to give you lots of ideas for quick and easy food to fit all your moods and to match your favourite programmes. Trailers like Spiced nuts, Popcorn and Cheese and walnut crescents whet the appetite for main features that include such delights as North sea cobbler, Sunny spice eggs and Bavarian sausage râgout. For a quick break try one of our soups, pâtés or pizzas while in supporting roles we have lots of delicious vegetable ideas. There's always a happy ending with Chocolate fudge pudding, Spicy peaches or Magical muesli cookies. Finally, wind down and switch off with a Hot malted sleepmaker or St Clement's cup.

So pick your programme, choose your recipe and settle down for refreshment of body and soul. With this book at your fingertips, your TV Dinners will always be top of the ratings.

HOW TO USE THIS BOOK

You will find the following information and symbols used throughout the book:

Preparation and Cooking Times

This information will help you to plan your meals around your favourite programmes. Many of the dishes are very quick to make, but those with longer cooking times can usually be left to cook on their own. You will often find that while one thing is cooking, the next stage can be prepared, thus cutting down time spent in the kitchen.

Symbols

This means that the completed dish is recommended for freezing. Some of the dishes can be frozen uncooked, in which case information will be given in the recipe. Make sure that you wrap the food well and take care when thawing and reheating.

This means that the food is suitable for vegetarians. In some recipes you may need to substitute one ingredient for another, in which case we have suggested an alternative in the introduction to the recipe.

This means that the recipe can be prepared from store cupboard ingredients. We give a suggested store cupboard shopping list which includes buying for the freezer (see pages 6 and 7). Where you see this symbol, the recipe can be cooked from ingredients on this list.

Measures

Use either Metric or Imperial measures, but do not mix the two. All spoon measures are assumed to be level.

Microwave Instructions

The recipes have been tested on a 600 watt microwave, where HIGH power is 600 watts, MEDIUM power is 360 watts and LOW power is 180 watts. If your oven differs from this, adjust the timing accordingly. DO remember to use utensils suitable for your microwave. Instructions for cooking in a combination oven have not been included since variations in the many models on the market would have made it impossible to generalise. Many of the dishes will cook well in a combination oven, however. For timings, consult your manufacturer's handbook, if possible locating a similar recipe as a guide to converting recipes. Where we feel a recipe is unsuitable for cooking in a microwave or where the result is not as good as with conventional methods, we have said so. We do not believe in sacrificing quality for speed and would rather spend a little extra time to produce a better result.

Tips

At the end of some recipes you will find tips, gleaned from years of experience in the kitchen. These relate directly to the recipe or may offer variations.

USEFUL STORE CUPBOARD INGREDIENTS

A good store cupboard is invaluable and can form the base of many recipes with just the addition of a single fresh ingredient; indeed there are recipes which can be created entirely from items in the store cupboard. As a refrigerator and freezer are so commonplace these days we have included them as part of our store cupboard.

Dry Store

flour, plain and self-raising, white and wholemeal; cornflour; sugar, white and brown; rice; pasta and instant Chinese noodles; dried or canned beans, e.g. kidney, haricot, borlotti; breakfast cereals, including muesli; bread mix; popcorn kernels; coffee; tea; drinking chocolate; cocoa; nuts; dried fruit; baking powder; golden syrup; jam; dried milk; chocolate; oil, sunflower and olive.

Sauces and Flavourings

mayonnaise; soy sauce; tomato ketchup and purée; pickle; Worcestershire sauce; lemon juice; pesto; yeast extract, beef extract or vegetable extract; stock powder or cubes; salt and black pepper; garlic paste; curry powder or paste; mustard, powder and prepared; selection of your favourite herbs and spices.

Canned Goods

tuna in brine or water; beans (not the baked variety); tomatoes; sweetcorn; soups; fruit in natural juice; canned fruit pie filling.

Freezer

puff pastry; filo pastry; rubbed-in shortcrust pastry; bread, breadcrumbs; peas; mixed peppers; sweetcorn; boil-in-the-bag fish; minced beef; ice cream; parsley; grated cheese; bacon.

Refrigerator

butter; eggs; margarine; lard; milk; fruit juice; Iceberg lettuce; cream in an aerosol; German-style sausage.

NOTE: Eggs should only be bought from a reputable supplier. Do not use cracked eggs; avoid serving foods made from raw eggs to the very young or the very old; and store eggs in the refrigerator, bringing them to room temperature immediately before use.

Vegetable Basket

fresh fruit; fresh vegetables including onions, garlic, potatoes.

STORING FOOD

The main rule here is *Clean*, *cool* and *covered*.

● Now that the amount of preservatives in many foods has been reduced, it is even more important to take care in storage. Perishable foods should be stored below 7°C (44°F) to prevent growth of bacteria. Remember that bacteria can multiply rapidly – within 24 hours a few bacteria can become several million.

● Food stored in the refrigerator should always be covered. Make sure that raw and cooked foods are stored separately. Clean out the refrigerator regularly, and throw away any dubious leftovers.

● In the past many houses had a pantry which was well ventilated and cool. Most modern homes only have storage cupboards, so many more ingredients need to be stored in the refrigerator, including some jams, sauces and vegetables.

PREPARING, THAWING, COOKING AND REHEATING

● Always wash hands before starting to prepare foods; cover any cuts with a clean, waterproof dressing. Chopping boards can harbour bacteria: sterilise frequently and never cut up cooked food on a board which has been used for raw meat or poultry.

● Allow food to thaw thoroughly before cooking.

● Cook food for long enough and at high enough temperatures for harmful bacteria to be killed.

● Always reheat thoroughly, again bringing the food to a temperature which will kill any harmful bacteria. Only reheat food once.

A TV GOURMET'S GUIDE TO EATING

There can be pitfalls in eating while engrossed in your favourite programme. A nailbiting car chase could result in spaghetti on the sofa, a passionate love scene could melt the ice cream and a sudden gunshot in a gripping thriller could leave the tray on the floor and the food in your lap!

Most of the food in this book may be eaten with fingers, fork or spoon. You may find a tray and a large napkin help, or if you are going to take this really seriously a folding TV table could prove invaluable.

Have all trays or tables set up in advance, with cutlery, condiments and liquid refreshment and don't forget a coin – to toss for who goes back to the kitchen for anything forgotten!

TRAILERS

*T*his section contains snacks and nibbles which are small and exciting, just as any good trailer should be. Lucky dip, Spiced nuts or Gentleman's twists will really whet the appetite and put everyone in the mood for the main feature. Don't reserve these recipes exclusively for trailers however; serve a selection at a party and watch them become the main attraction.

CROSTINI AND CROUSTADES

Makes 24 / Preparation: 10 minutes / Cooking: 10 minutes

Crostini are small cut-out bread shapes which may be either deep fried or baked and then used as a base for a variety of toppings. Croustades are shapes of either bread or pastry which are moulded into tartlet shapes and baked or prepared like vols-au-vent so that they can then be filled. We have chosen to bake both crostini and croustades; flavour them with garlic if you like – this makes them especially good. Once baked, allow them to cool, then store in an airtight container. They will keep for a week or so. For a quick snack, simply add toppings of your own choice – pâté, cheese, potted shrimps, etc. We have made small shapes, but this may of course be varied.

6 large slices of bread
25 g (1 oz) butter, softened
1 clove garlic, crushed (optional)
fat for greasing

1. Cut each slice of bread into 4 rounds using a plain 5 cm (2 in) cutter.
2. Beat the butter and garlic in a bowl, then spread over the rounds of bread.
3. For crostini, arrange on a greased baking sheet; for croustades, press into greased bun tins. Bake in a preheated oven at 220°C (425°F), Gas Mark 7 for 10 minutes or until golden brown.

MICROWAVE: not suitable. The butter however could be softened on LOW power.

SALTED SUNFLOWER SEEDS

Makes 50 g (2 oz) / Preparation: 5 minutes / Cooking: 5–10 minutes

This is a high protein snack, fairly cheap to make and a change from nuts. A word of warning: they remain hot for a surprisingly long while – give them time to cool down and avoid burning your mouth!

15 ml (1 tbsp) sunflower oil
50 g (2 oz) sunflower seeds
salt to taste

1. Heat the oil in a frying pan and add the sunflower seeds. Fry gently for a few minutes until they are evenly browned.
2. Tip the seeds on to a piece of absorbent kitchen paper to drain, then transfer to a bowl. Add salt to taste. Serve when cold.

MINI QUICHES

Makes 24 / Preparation: 20 minutes / Cooking: 20 minutes

Large slices of quiche can be difficult to eat and are often rather soggy when frozen and reheated. These little quiches however, are easy to eat and freeze extremely well. It is a good idea to make a batch and store them in layers in a plastic container in the freezer. That way, you can simply take out the number you want at any time and pop them straight into the oven to reheat. They make an ideal snack. We give you a Quiche Lorraine filling, but 350 g (12 oz) of any other filling such as flaked poached smoked haddock or chopped asparagus could be used equally well. Do feel free to use a frozen pastry – the wholemeal ones available now are very good. Omit the bacon when cooking for vegetarians and use suitable fat and cheese.

PASTRY
225 g (8 oz) plain flour
pinch of salt
125 g (4 oz) margarine or margarine and white fat
45 ml (3 tbsp) cold water

FILLING
10 ml (2 tsp) oil
125 g (4 oz) smoked streaky bacon, finely chopped
125 g (4 oz) onion, finely chopped
125 g (4 oz) Cheddar cheese, finely grated
2 eggs
300 ml (½ pt) milk
salt and freshly ground black pepper

1. Sift the flour and salt into a bowl and rub in the fat until the mixture resembles fine breadcrumbs. Stir in the water, then knead together lightly to form a smooth dough.
2. Roll out the pastry on a floured surface and use to line bun tins. You should make approximately 24 quiche cases.
3. Heat the oil in a frying pan and gently cook the bacon and onion until soft. Using a teaspoon, divide between the pastry cases. Top each with a teaspoon of grated cheese.
4. Beat the eggs, milk and seasoning in a bowl or jug and carefully pour into each pastry case. Bake in a preheated oven at 200°C (400°F), Gas Mark 6 for about 20 minutes or until goldn brown. Remove from the tins and serve hot or cold. *(cont.)*

MICROWAVE: the quiches are not suitable for baking in a microwave, but this appliance may be used to cook the base for the filling. Place the oil, bacon and onion in a bowl and cook on HIGH power for 4 minutes, stirring occasionally.

BUTTERY CHEESE BISCUITS

Makes 30 / Preparation: 10 minutes plus chilling / Cooking: 10–15 minutes

These light and crumbly biscuits will have your friends asking for the recipe. It is essential to use butter if the biscuits are to be light and flaky. Keep a little of the dough in the refrigerator ready to roll out. Better still, prepare the biscuits to the end of step 3, open freeze on baking sheets, wrap when frozen and cook when required.

175 g (6 oz) butter
175 g (6 oz) Cheddar cheese, finely grated
175 g (6 oz) plain flour
pinch of mustard powder
a little beaten egg for glazing

1. Put all the ingredients except the egg into a mixer or food processor and mix to a smooth firm dough.
2. Wrap the dough in cling film and refrigerate for 1 hour.
3. Roll out half the dough at a time on a floured board to a thickness of 5 mm (¼ in). Cut into shapes.
4. Place the shapes on a baking sheet and brush with beaten egg. Bake in a preheated oven at 190°C (375°F), Gas Mark 5 for 10–15 minutes or until golden.
5. Remove carefully from the sheet and cool on a wire rack. They are very crumbly.

YORK FINGERS

Serves 6 / Preparation: 10 minutes / Cooking: 10 minutes

These get their name from the York ham originally used as a filling. Any type of ham works equally well. If you have any leftovers, they will do fine. The pastries may be frozen after baking for reheating when required, or at the end of step 4 for cooking from frozen. Open freeze, then pack in a plastic box.

225 g (8 oz) puff pastry
15 ml (1 tbsp) mild mustard or to taste
50 g (2 oz) ham, finely diced
175 g (6 oz) Cheddar cheese, finely grated
beaten egg for glazing

1. On a floured board roll out the pastry to a large rectangle 5 mm (¼ in) thick.
2. Spread half the pastry thinly with the mustard; sprinkle on the ham and cheese.
3. Fold the pastry in half and roll out again to seal in the filling.
4. Brush with the egg, cut into fingers about 2.5 × 7.5 cm (1 × 3 in) and place on a baking sheet.
5. Bake in a preheated oven at 220°C (425°F), Gas Mark 7 for about 10 minutes or until puffy and golden.

LUCKY DIP

Serves 4 / Preparation: 10 minutes

A simple, but more-ish dip which always has guests guessing at the ingredients. It should be served with a selection of crudites (fresh vegetable sticks). The dip may be adapted to form the basis of a main course by the addition of shelled cooked prawns and a salad.

75 ml (5 tbsp) mayonnaise
15 ml (1 tbsp) tomato ketchup
dash of Worcestershire sauce
squeeze of lemon juice
10 ml (2 tsp) finely chopped onion
2 tomatoes, chopped
15 ml (1 tbsp) chopped capers (optional)
salt and freshly ground black pepper

1. Mix together all the ingredients and place in a bowl. Serve with crudites – fresh sticks of carrot, cucumber, celery, green or red pepper etc.

PESTO AND MOZZARELLA TOASTS

Makes 2 / Preparation: 5 minutes / Cooking: 5 minutes

This is a more exciting version of cheese on toast. Although the ingredients sound exotic they are becoming readily available. Pesto is usually a mixture of basil, garlic, olive oil, grated Parmesan cheese and pine nuts pounded together. You can make it yourself or buy it in a jar from a large supermarket or delicatessen. It makes a good sauce for spaghetti. Mozzarella cheese, a traditional pizza topping, is usually sold in a plastic bag because it is kept in water. Cheddar would be an acceptable substitute.

6 slices of French bread
10 ml (2 tsp) pesto
125 g (4 oz) Mozzarella cheese, sliced
a few almonds or pine nuts to garnish

1. Toast the bread on both sides under a preheated grill.
2. Spread each slice thinly with pesto and top with a slice of cheese and a few nuts.
3. Return to the grill until the cheese is bubbling. Serve immediately.

CHEESE AND WALNUT CRESCENTS

**Makes 16/ Preparation: 15 minutes plus chilling /
Cooking: 15 minutes**

These rich crescents are ideal for nibbling on their own. Alternatively, serve them as a starter with a mixed leaf salad with mustardy dressing. They may be cooked from frozen (freeze at the end of step 4) or reheated once cooked. Omit the ham and increase the quantity of nuts and they become suitable for vegetarians.

125 g (4 oz) cream cheese
125 g (4 oz) butter, softened
150 g (5 oz) plain flour

FILLING
1 egg, beaten
5 ml (1 tsp) prepared mild mustard
50 g (2 oz) ham, very finely chopped
75 g (3 oz) Cheddar cheese, finely grated
25 g (1 oz) walnuts, finely chopped

1. Beat the cream cheese and butter together in a mixing bowl. Gradually work in the flour. Form into a ball, wrap in cling film and chill for an hour or so until firm.
2. Roll out the dough on a floured board to a circle 40 cm (16 in) in diameter. Brush with some of the beaten egg.
3. Spread with the mustard and sprinkle with the ham, cheese and nuts, pressing the filling well into the pastry.
4. Cut the circle into 16 equal wedges. Starting from the wider end, roll each wedge up loosely, then bend each to form a crescent (see illustration below).
5. Place the crescents on a baking sheet and brush with egg. Bake in a preheated oven at 200°C (400°F), Gas Mark 6 for 12–15 minutes or until golden. Serve warm.

POPCORN

Serves 2–4 / Preparation and Cooking: 5 minutes

Arrange your seating in rows and pretend you are at the cinema! Sit back and enjoy the film while nibbling away at a bag of home-made popcorn. It is great fun to make – just be sure to have a saucepan lid at the ready before you begin, as the corn really jumps. Sprinkle the corn with salt while still in the saucepan; for sweet popcorn, sprinkle with sugar or coat in caramel.

15 ml (1 tbsp) oil
50 g (2 oz) popcorn kernels
salt or sugar

1. Heat the oil in a large saucepan and have the lid ready. Tip in the corn and cover with the lid.
2. Cook over a high heat until the corn begins to pop, then turn down the heat to medium and continue cooking until the popping stops. Sprinkle with salt or sugar while still hot.

MICROWAVE: place the popcorn kernels with the oil in a large covered casserole and heat on HIGH power for 7–8 minutes, shaking the dish occasionally. You may find that some corn has failed to pop. Look out for microwave-suitable popcorn which is cooked in its own bag.

GENTLEMAN'S TWISTS

Makes about 40 / Preparation: 10 minutes / Cooking: 10 minutes

A delicious nibble that is both quick and easy to prepare.

225 g (8 oz) frozen puff pastry
a little beef or vegetable extract or Gentleman's Relish

1. Roll out the pastry on a floured board to a large rectangle 5 mm (¼ in) thick.
2. Spread thinly with the extract or relish.
3. Cut into 15 × 1 cm (6 × ½ in) strips and twist.
4. Place on a baking sheet and bake in a preheated oven at 220°C (425°F), Gas Mark 7 for 7–10 minutes or until puffy and golden. Serve immediately.

SPICED NUTS

Makes 225 g (8 oz) / Preparation: 5 minutes / Cooking: 20 minutes

Unroasted nuts are usually considerably cheaper than roasted, so this is an economical way of providing a popular and nutritious nibble. Store these in an airtight jar, preferably hidden at the back of a cupboard if you want any left for you!

1 egg white
5 ml (1 tsp) sunflower oil
5 ml (1 tsp) salt
5 ml (1 tsp) paprika
225 g (8 oz) unroasted nuts, cashews, almonds, peanuts, hazelnuts or a mixture

1. Beat the egg white lightly in a large bowl. Stir in the oil, salt and paprika, then the nuts. Stir until the nuts are all well coated.
2. Spread on a baking sheet and bake in a preheated oven at 150°C (300°F), Gas Mark 2 for 20 minutes, turning the nuts over once or twice. They should be brown and crisp.

QUICK
BREAKS

When time is short and you don't feel like a full meal, you'll find something to suit here. This section contains satisfying snacks and light meals that can often be prepared in a commercial break but whose enjoyment will last throughout the evening. There are chunky soups for *soup*erstars, pâtés and mousses for big softies, and serious sandwiches for documentary lovers. All proving that a quick break need not be boring but can be as exciting as the latest big budget thriller.

FRESH VEGETABLE SOUP

Serves 6 / Preparation: 15 minutes / Cooking: 20 minutes

A good, wholesome vegetable soup which makes a filling meal when served with chunks of bread and a wedge of cheese. It is a good idea to keep a supply of fresh stock in the freezer. This can easily be made by boiling chicken bones in water to cover and then simmering for an hour or so. Strain the stock and bag up in usable quantities. Failing this, a stock cube will of course suffice. For a creamier vegetable soup, use half milk and half stock and purée before serving.

10 ml (2 tsp) oil
1 onion, finely chopped
2 sticks celery, chopped
1 leek, washed thoroughly and chopped
225 g (8 oz) carrots, scraped and chopped
1 large potato, peeled and chopped
1.2 litres (2 pt) chicken or vegetable stock
salt and freshly ground black pepper

1. Heat the oil in a large saucepan and stir in all the vegetables. Cover and sweat for 5 minutes over a low heat, shaking the pan occasionally.
2. Pour over the stock and bring to the boil. Lower the heat, cover and simmer for 15–20 minutes or until the vegetables are tender. Season to taste. Serve at once or reheat during that commercial break.

MICROWAVE: as this is a large quantity of soup it would take longer to cook in the microwave than by conventional means, so it is better cooked on the hob.

GERMAN PEA SOUP

Serves 6 / Preparation: 10 minutes / Cooking: 30 minutes

This is a very substantial soup, a meal in itself. If you don't have a blender, serve it as it comes, but take a little more care with the cutting of the vegetables. For vegetarians, omit the sausages and serve sprinkled with grated cheese.

350 g (12 oz) frozen peas
6 spring onions, sliced
2 carrots, scraped and diced
225 g (8 oz) potato, peeled and diced
5 ml (1 tsp) sugar
1.2 litres (2 pt) vegetable stock
225 g (8 oz) German sausage in a piece
salt and freshly ground black pepper to taste

1. Place all the ingredients except the seasoning in a saucepan. Bring to the boil, lower the heat, cover and simmer for 30 minutes.
2. Remove the sausage and reserve. Purée the soup in a blender or food processor or push through a sieve into a clean saucepan.
3. Season the soup to taste, adding additional stock if it is too thick. Slice the sausage and add it to the soup. Reheat before serving.

MICROWAVE: follow the above directions but cook the soup in a casserole for 10 minutes on HIGH power, then for 10 minutes on MEDIUM power.

TIP: if you want to serve this as a vegetable accompaniment omit the sausage and the stock, substituting 25 g (1 oz) butter and 15 ml (1 tbsp) water. Bake it in a covered casserole in a preheated oven at 180°C (350°F), Gas Mark 4 for 40 minutes or until the carrots are tender. This time may vary according to how cold the peas are.

MUSHROOM SOUP

Serves 4 / Preparation: 5 minutes / Cooking: 15 minutes

A delicious, creamy soup made in minutes. You will never open a can again! The basic soup can of course be adapted to other flavours, for example by adding canned asparagus or sweetcorn instead of mushrooms. Use small, tight button mushrooms for the best result.

25 g (1 oz) butter or margarine
25 g (1 oz) plain flour
300 ml (½ pt) milk
300 ml (½ pt) chicken or vegetable stock
125 g (4 oz) button mushrooms, wiped and thinly sliced
squeeze of lemon juice
salt and freshly ground black pepper

1. Place the butter, flour, milk and stock in a medium saucepan and bring to the boil, whisking constantly. Boil for 2 minutes.
2. Stir in the mushrooms, lemon juice and seasoning. Return to the boil, then lower the heat, cover and simmer for 10–15 minutes. Serve at once.

MICROWAVE: melt the butter in a medium casserole on HIGH power for 1 minute. Stir in the flour, then gradually whisk in the milk and stock (use boiling stock). Stir in the mushrooms, lemon juice and seasoning, cover and cook on HIGH power for 10 minutes, stirring occasionally.

TIP: keep a jar of vegetable stock paste or powder in the store cupboard. You will find it invaluable for making quick soups or savoury hot drinks.

SWEETCORN CHOWDER

Serves 4 / Preparation and Cooking: 20 minutes

Serve this thick soup with wholemeal bread for a meal that's as wholesome as it is hearty. Use the sweetcorn with chopped pimiento for extra colour or for a change substitute flaked poached smoked haddock for the cottage cheese.

25 g (1 oz) butter
1 onion, finely chopped
25 g (1 oz) plain flour
450 ml (¾ pt) milk
150 ml (¼ pt) chicken or vegetable stock
225 g (8 oz) sweetcorn, canned or frozen
15 ml (1 tbsp) chopped parsley
225 g (8 oz) cottage cheese
salt and freshly ground black pepper

1. Melt the butter in a large saucepan and gently fry the onion until soft. Stir in the flour, then gradually whisk in the milk and stock. Bring to the boil, stirring constantly.
2. Stir in the sweetcorn. Bring back to the boil, then lower the heat, cover and simmer for 10–15 minutes.
3. Stir in the parsley, cottage cheese and seasoning and reheat gently before serving. Do not allow to boil.

MICROWAVE: melt the butter on HIGH power for 1 minute, then stir in the onion. Cook on HIGH power for 3 minutes, stir in the flour then whisk in the hot milk and stock. Stir in the sweetcorn, cover and cook on HIGH power for 10–12 minutes, stirring occasionally. Finally stir in the parsley, cottage cheese and seasoning and cook on HIGH power for 3–4 minutes or until reheated.

KIPPER PÂTÉ

Serves 6 / Preparation and Cooking: 15 minutes plus chilling

A really useful pâté, good enough to serve as a starter at a dinner party, but simple enough for a quick TV snack. Smoked mackerel could be used instead to avoid the necessity for cooking the fish or try poached smoked haddock for a change. The pâté will keep in the refrigerator for two days and is delicious spread on warm toast.

225 g (8 oz) frozen boil-in-the-bag kipper fillets
50 g (2 oz) butter
1 small onion, finely chopped
125 g (4 oz) cream cheese
10 ml (2 tsp) lemon juice
salt and freshly ground black pepper

1. Cook the kippers according to the instructions on the packet, then skin and flake the fish with a fork.
2. Melt the butter in a saucepan and gently fry the onion until soft. Remove from the heat and beat in the flaked fish with the remaining ingredients. Spoon into a dish and chill in the refrigerator for at least 1 hour.

MICROWAVE: cook the kipper fillets according to the instructions on the packet. Melt the butter with the onion in a covered dish on HIGH power for 3 minutes. Beat in the fish and remaining ingredients, then chill as above.

RED LENTIL AND PARSLEY PÂTÉ

Serves 4 / Preparation and Cooking: 20 minutes plus chilling

Quick to make, quick to spread and quick to eat! That certainly describes this pâté which will be enjoyed by vegetarians and non-vegetarians alike. Vary it by using green lentils instead of red or by adding chives instead of parsley.

125 g (4 oz) red lentils
300 ml (½ pt) water
50 g (2 oz) butter
15 ml (1 tbsp) chopped parsley
5 ml (1 tsp) lemon juice
salt and freshly ground black pepper

1. Rinse the lentils, then place in a saucepan with the water. Cover and simmer for 10–15 minutes or until the mixture resembles a thick purée.
2. Beat in the butter, parsley, lemon juice and seasoning. Spoon into a dish, smooth the surface and chill in the refrigerator for at least 1 hour or until firm.

MICROWAVE: rinse the lentils and place in a large casserole with the water. Cook uncovered on HIGH power for 8–10 minutes, adding a little more water if necessary, until a thick purée is formed. Proceed from step 2 of the method.

CHEESE PÂTÉ

Serves 6–8 / Preparation: 10 minutes

Make a double quantity of this nutritious pâté and keep it in the refrigerator. You will be amazed how many different uses you will find for it: a quick topping for crackers, a sandwich spread, a topping for baked jacket potatoes. Add a little plain yogurt and it becomes a dip for fresh vegetable sticks. Blue cheese may be used instead of Cheddar.

50 g (2 oz) butter, softened
225 g (8 oz) Cheddar cheese, finely grated
5 ml (1 tsp) prepared mustard
15 ml (1 tbsp) top-of-the-milk or cream
freshly ground black pepper

1. Combine all the ingredients in a bowl and mix to a smooth paste with a wooden spoon. Transfer to a serving dish, level the surface, cover with cling film and keep in the refrigerator until required.

MUSHROOM MOUSSE

Serves 6 / Preparation and Cooking: 20 minutes plus chilling

This is a delicious starter or supper dish which will benefit from being prepared well in advance. It tastes rich but is relatively low in calories. Serve it with crispbreads, crudites or hot toast.

1 × 425 g (15 oz) can beef or game consommé
175 g (6 oz) button mushrooms, wiped and sliced
½ × 11 g (⅓ oz) sachet gelatine
225 g (8 oz) skimmed milk or low fat soft cheese
1 clove garlic, crushed
1.25 ml (¼ tsp) grated nutmeg
15 ml (1 tbsp) chopped parsley

1. Heat 60 ml (4 tbsp) of the consommé in a small saucepan over gentle heat until melted. Add the mushrooms and poach for 2 minutes. Set aside until cool.
2. Drain the mushroom liquid into a cup and sprinkle on the gelatine. Set aside for 2 minutes until spongy, then stand the cup in a saucepan of boiling water until all the gelatine has dissolved.
3. Reserve half the remaining consommé. Pour the rest into a bowl. Add the milk or cheese with the garlic, nutmeg and parsley. Whisk well until smooth. Add half the liquid gelatine.
4. Reserve 6 of the best mushroom slices. Stir the remainder into the cheese mixture, spoon into 6 ramekins and chill for about 1 hour.
5. Meanwhile combine the reserved liquid gelatine and the remaining consommé in a small saucepan. Set aside.
6. When the mousses are set place a mushroom slice on top of each. Warm the gelatine and consommé mixture gently until it liquifies – do not allow it to become hot. Gently flood the surface of each mousse with the liquid gelatine to form a thin layer. Return to the refrigerator for at lest 45 minutes until set.

MICROWAVE: the mushrooms may be cooked for 2 minutes on HIGH power in a covered dish. After soaking the gelatine may be melted in 30 seconds to 1 minute on HIGH power.

TUNA AND CHIVE-STUFFED JACKET POTATOES

Serves 4 / Preparation: 10 minutes / Cooking: 1½ hours

This simple lunch or supper dish uses mainly store cupboard ingredients so is ideal for unexpected guests. The cooking time can be cut considerably if the potatoes are baked in a microwave or combination oven.

4 large baking potatoes
1 × 198 g (7 oz) can tuna in brine, drained and flaked
25 g (1 oz) butter, melted
50 g (2 oz) Edam cheese, finely grated
60 ml (4 tbsp) single cream
10 ml (2 tsp) lemon juice
15 ml (1 tbsp) dry sherry
15 ml (1 tbsp) chopped fresh chives or 5 ml (1 tsp) dried chives
salt and freshly ground black pepper

1. Scrub the potatoes and bake in their jackets in a preheated oven at 180°C (350°F), Gas Mark 4 for about 1½ hours or until soft.
2. Meanwhile place the flaked tuna in a bowl. Add all the other ingredients except the salt and pepper and beat thoroughly with a wooden spoon to a smooth paste.
3. Season to taste, using very little salt but plenty of black pepper.
4. When the potatoes are cooked, transfer them to a serving dish. Cut a deep cross incision in the top of each. Squeeze gently from opposing sides and the cuts should open up like the petals of a flower.
5. Fill the centre of each potato with tuna mixture and return to the oven for 10 minutes or until the filling is hot. Serve immediately.

MICROWAVE: prick the potatoes and cook on HIGH power for about 15 minutes or until the potatoes are soft. Turn once during the cooking time. Fill and return to the microwave for 4 minutes on HIGH power.

TOASTED SANDWICHES

Serves any number / Preparation: 10–15 minutes

We couldn't ignore toasted sandwiches in our suggestions for simple snacks. Devotees will have their favourite fillings and will plug in toasted sandwich makers as readily as they will turn on the TV. For the uninitiated, here's how to make these substantial treats with nothing more sophisticated than a grill. We have not given quantities, as this is best left to your own judgement.

medium sliced bread
butter or margarine

FILLINGS
(Choose one of the following)
cheese and onion
cheese and cooked slice ham
cheese, tomato and chopped chives
sardines, lemon juice and seasoning
cooked ham, pineapple and cheese
frankfurters and pickle
baked beans
scrambled egg and mushrooms
cheese, apple and cinnamon
banana and grated chocolate

1. Preheat the grill to high.
2. Butter the bread on both sides, then sandwich together with one of the above fillings.
3. Place in the grill pan, grill on one side until lightly browned, then turn over carefully and grill the second side.

BAKED BAGUETTES

Serves 4 / Preparation: 5 minutes / Cooking: 10 minutes

Hot, spicy and substantial – the perfect snack for armchair sportsmen.

2 small baguettes or French sticks
about 45 ml (3 tbsp) softened butter
about 30 ml (2 tbsp) mustard relish
4 slices, about 125 g (4 oz) Emmental cheese, halved
4 slices, about 125 g (4 oz) cooked ham, halved

1. Cut 4 diagonal slits in each baguette, taking care to avoid slicing through the bottom crust.
2. Spread about 5 ml (1 tsp) butter into each slit and add some mustard relish.
3. Tuck a slice of cheese and a slice of ham into each slit, then wrap the sticks in foil. Bake in a preheated oven at 190°C (375°F), Gas Mark 5 for 10 minutes or until the cheese melts.
4. Remove from the foil and cut each baguette in half to serve.

TURKISH PEDE

Serves 4 / Preparation: 15 minutes / Cooking: 15–20 minutes

This recipe was picked up in a Pede Parlour on a Turkish beach. It is absolutely delicious and easy to make using a bread mix from the store cupboard. This dish can be cooked in advance and reheated in a hot oven. Pede is traditionally cooked in a brick oven which is never allowed to go out, which is why we recommend such a high temperature.

1 × 280 g (10 oz) packet bread mix
225 g (8 oz) lean minced beef
225 g (8 oz) onions, finely chopped
225 g (8 oz) tomatoes, finely chopped
60 ml (4 tbsp) Greek parsley, chopped or
90 ml (6 tbsp) English parsley, chopped
salt and freshly ground black pepper
2 eggs
60 ml (4 tbsp) water
oil for greasing

1. Make a bread dough, following the directions on the packet. Divide the dough into four and roll each piece out to a long thin boat shape about 30 × 13 cm (12 × 5 in).
2. Place the dough shapes on greased baking sheets.
3. In a bowl, mix the beef, onions, tomatoes, parsley and seasoning. The easiest way to do this is to use clean hands.
4. Spread a quarter of the mixture on each bread base, turning up the sides of the dough to contain the juices (see illustration below).
5. Bake in a preheated oven set to maximum heat, at least 220°C (450°F), Gas Mark 8 for 10–15 minutes.
6. Meanwhile beat the eggs with the water in a measuring jug with salt and pepper to taste. Remove the boats from the oven, pour over the egg and return to the oven for about 5 minutes more. The egg should be just set.
7. Serve hot, cut into slices.

SPAGHETTI CARBONARA

Serves 4 / Preparation and Cooking: 20 minutes

This is the genuine article – the recipe was given to us by a local woman we met while staying in Italy. Unfortunately, the deliciously-flavoured Italian bacon is not easy to obtain here, but a good smoked back bacon is an acceptable substitute.

225 g (8 oz) spaghetti
15 ml (1 tbsp) oil
25 g (1 oz) butter
225 g (8 oz) smoked back bacon, rind removed, chopped
300 ml (½ pt) double cream
2 egg yolks
salt and freshly ground black pepper
50 g (2 oz) freshly grated Parmesan cheese

1. Bring a large saucepan of salted water to the boil. Add the spaghetti and oil, return to the boil, then cover the pan and remove from the heat. Leave to stand for 12 minutes or until cooked but still firm to the bite.
2. Meanwhile melt the butter in a large frying pan and fry the bacon until lightly crisped. In a jug, beat together the cream, egg yolks and seasoning. Pour into the frying pan and heat gently, stirring constantly until the mixture has thickened slightly.
3. Drain the pasta and divide between warm serving plates. Pour over the sauce and serve, sprinkled with freshly grated Parmesan.

MICROWAVE: follow step 1. Place 15 g (½ oz) butter only in a casserole with the bacon and cook on HIGH power for 3 minutes, stirring occasionally. Beat the cream, egg yolks and seasoning together, then pour over the bacon. Cook on HIGH power for 3 minutes, stirring frequently. Serve as described above.

PASTA WITH PARSLEY AND WALNUT SAUCE

Serves 2 / Preparation and Cooking: 20 minutes

This sophisticated pasta dish is ideal for vegetarians. Prepare everything in advance and you can cook it in little more time than it takes for a commercial break. Eat it Italian-style, with a spoon and fork. If you are serving it on trays, choose pasta shapes in preference to spaghetti or tagliatelle and avoid loose ends. Used as a starter, it will serve four.

175 g (6 oz) pasta: noodles, tagliatelle or shapes
75 ml (5 tbsp) sunflower oil
25 g (1 oz) margarine
75 g (3 oz) walnuts, roughly chopped
75 ml (5 tbsp) fresh brown breadcrumbs
grated rind and juice of 1 lemon
60 ml (4 tbsp) chopped parsley
salt and freshly ground black pepper

1. Bring a large saucepan of salted water to the boil. Add the pasta, and 15 ml (1 tbsp) of the oil. Return to the boil, then stir, cover the pan and remove from the heat. Leave to stand for 10–12 minutes or until cooked but still firm to the bite.
2. Meanwhile melt the margarine in a frying pan. Fry the walnuts for 1 minute, add the breadcrumbs and cook for 1 minute more, stirring constantly.
3. Gradually stir in the remaining oil and the grated lemon rind and juice. Purée, if desired, in a blender or food processor. Return to the clean pan and add the parsley. Season to taste and reheat gently.
4. Drain the pasta and place it in a heated serving dish. Pour over the sauce, mix gently and serve.

MICROWAVE: it is easier and as quick to cook the pasta on the hob, but the sauce may be made in the microwave. Combine the margarine and walnuts in a bowl and cook for 1 minute on HIGH power, then add the breadcrumbs and cook for 1 minute more, stirring twice. Proceed as from step 3 above.

OLIVE'S PASTA BAKE

Serves 2 / Preparation: 10 minutes / Cooking: 1¼ hours

This recipe was given to us by a friend. She assured us it worked, but we had our doubts. It looked much too dry; we thought it would never cook. However it does, and very delicious it is too. It takes very little time to prepare and can happily be left unsupervised while you settle down to watch a film. A green salad is the ideal accompaniment.

30 ml (2 tbsp) oil
2 onions, chopped
1 clove garlic, crushed
75 g (3 oz) spaghetti, broken into 7.5 cm (3 in) lengths
1 × 400 g (14 oz) can chopped tomatoes
salt and freshly ground black pepper
5 ml (1 tsp) dried oregano
175 g (6 oz) Cheddar cheese, grated
fat for greasing

1. Heat the oil in a saucepan, add the onions and garlic and cook gently until soft.
2. Grease an ovenproof dish and spread half the onion and garlic mixture on the base. Sprinkle over half the spaghetti followed by half the tomatoes, the seasoning and all the oregano. Top with the remaining onion mixture, rest of the spaghetti and lastly the remaining tomatoes.
3. Sprinkle with the cheese, patting it down gently, cover and cook in a preheated oven at 150°C (300°F), Gas Mark 2 for 1¼ hours.

SOUFFLÉ OMELETTE WITH HAM AND CHEESE

Serves 2 / Preparation: 5 minutes / Cooking: 6 minutes

This is much more exciting than an ordinary omelette, yet can be made quickly and easily. Do make sure the grill is really hot or the omelette will toughen. Toppings may be savoury or sweet. For alternative fillings, try smoked haddock and cheese, or mushrooms, or jam for a quick dessert.

3 large eggs
30 ml (2 tbsp) milk
salt and freshly ground black pepper
15 g (½ oz) butter
50 g (2 oz) Cheddar cheese, grated
50 g (2 oz) ham, cut into strips

1. Preheat the grill.
2. Separate the eggs. Beat the yolks with the milk and seasoning. In a separate bowl, whisk the egg whites until stiff, then fold into the yolk mixture.
3. Melt the butter in a good non-stick frying pan which may be used under the grill. Pour in the egg mixture and cook over moderate heat until the omelette is nearly set.
4. Sprinkle on the cheese and ham and grill until lightly browned. Serve and eat immediately.

MICROWAVE: cook in a 20 cm (8 in) flan dish. Follow steps 1 and 2 above, then melt the butter on HIGH power for 30 seconds and spread around the flan dish. Add the omelette mixture and microwave on HIGH power for 4 minutes, turning the dish around halfway through cooking. Top with the cheese and ham and grill as above.

TIP: if food sticks to your frying pan try proving it. Heat a little oil in the pan and add a lot of salt. Using a pad of absorbent kitchen paper rub the surface of the pan, taking care not to burn yourself. This gently scours and seals a pan and will usually improve it considerably. Do not do this if your pan has a non-stick coating.

SAVOURY BAKED EGGS

Serves 4 / Preparation: 15 minutes / Cooking: 15–20 minutes

Just a little more interesting than the classic *oeufs en cocotte*, this recipe makes a swiftly prepared snack. Served with warm buttered fingers of toast its as easily digested as your favourite soap, but considerably more nutritious!

2 tomatoes
50 g (2 oz) button mushrooms, wiped and finely chopped
15 ml (1 tbsp) finely chopped onion
5 ml (1 tsp) basil
5 ml (1 tsp) chopped parsley
salt and freshly ground black pepper
4 eggs
45 ml (3 tbsp) single cream or top-of-the-milk
50 g (2 oz) Cheddar cheese, grated
butter for greasing

1. Skin the tomatoes: prick the skins, place the tomatoes in a bowl and add boiling water to cover. Leave for 2 minutes, then drain and remove the skins. Alternatively, skewer each tomato in turn on a fork and hold in a gas flame until the skin loosens. Peel.
2. Chop the tomatoes and place in a bowl with the mushrooms, onion, herbs and seasoning. Mix well. Divide between 4 buttered ramekins or individual dishes.
3. Break one egg into each dish, then spoon over the cream and sprinkle with cheese. Bake in a preheated oven at 180°C (350°F), Gas Mark 4 for 15–20 minutes.

BAKED HERBY EGGS

Makes 8 / Preparation: 15 minutes / Cooking: 30–35 minutes

This delicious variation on Scotch eggs is baked instead of fried, making it much tastier and also lower in fat. For a variation on this recipe, try replacing the egg with a knob of Jarlsberg or Gruyère cheese and baking in the same way. This will make between 12 and 16 herby cheeses.

4 hard-boiled eggs
450 g (1 lb) sausagemeat
75 g (3 oz) fresh white breadcrumbs
salt and freshly ground black pepper
2.5 ml (½ tsp) mixed dried herbs
oil for greasing

1. Cut the eggs in half widthways. Divide the sausagement into 8 equal portions.
2. Mix together the breadcrumbs, seasoning and herbs in a shallow dish.
3. Wrap each half egg in sausagemeat, making sure there are no gaps, then roll it in the breadcrumb mixture. Pat the breadcrumb coating on firmly.
4. Place the coated eggs on a greased baking sheet and bake in a preheated oven at 220°C (425°F), Gas Mark 7 for 30–35 minutes or until the coating is crisp and golden.

SPINACH AND SALMON ROULADE

Serves 2–3 / Preparation: 15 minutes plus chilling

This uncooked roulade can be assembled in minutes. Served in slices with a good mixed salad, it makes a light but appetising meal or dinner party starter. Make it as a long thin roll, slice it neatly and it makes a perfect topping for crostini (see page 8). If spinach is not available, use a small round lettuce instead.

225 g (8 oz) fresh spinach
1 × 200 g (7 oz) can pink salmon
125 g (4 oz) cream cheese
salt and freshly ground black pepper

1. Choose about 10 of the largest spinach leaves, remove the thickest part of the stalk, then wash.
2. Place the leaves in a bowl and cover with boiling water. Drain immediately, then plunge into cold water. Spread the leaves out on absorbent kitchen paper and gently pat dry.
3. Place a 20 cm (8 in) square sheet of greaseproof paper on a clean work surface and cover with the lettuce leaves, overlapping them so that all the paper is covered.
4. Drain the salmon, removing any skin and bones and place in a bowl. Add the cream cheese and seasoning and mix well. Carefully spread the mixture over the lettuce leaves.
5. Roll the lettuce leaves over the filling like a Swiss roll, using the greaseproof paper as a guide. Place the roulade on a plate and chill in the refrigerator for at least 1 hour before cutting into slices and serving.

KEDGEREE

**Serves 4 / Preparation: 10 minutes plus standing /
Cooking: 15–16 minutes**

This is much too good to save for its traditional breakfast slot. Serve it for lunch or supper, varying the amount of spice to suit personal tastes. It may be made in advance and reheated when required and is the perfect dish to serve when the action on TV is so fast that you can't take your eyes away from the screen. All you need to eat it is a fork and a good sense of direction.

350 g (12 oz) smoked haddock
60 ml (4 tbsp) water
50 g (2 oz) butter
1 large onion, chopped
225 g (8 oz) long-grain rice
5 ml (1 tbsp) turmeric
5 ml (1 tsp) mild curry powder or paste
salt and freshly ground black pepper
30 ml (2 tbsp) chopped parsley
2 hard-boiled eggs

1. Skin the fish and cut into chunks. Place the fish in a saucepan with the water. Bring to the boil, then cover, remove from the heat and leave to stand for 10 minutes. Test – the fish should flake when touched with the tip of a knife. If it is not ready bring to the boil again.
2. Melt half the butter in a saucepan and fry the onion until it begins to soften but not brown. Stir in the rice and the spices and fry for 2 minutes.
3. With a slotted spoon, transfer the fish to a bowl. Drain the liquid in which it was cooked into a measuring jug and make up to 600 ml (1 pt) with water. Add to the rice mixture.
4. Bring to the boil, then lower the heat, cover the pan and simmer very gently for 12 minutes. Stir and remove from the heat. Leave the lid on the pan for a further 10 minutes, by which time all the liquid should have been absorbed and the rice should be tender.
5. Flake the fish and stir it into the rice mixture, with the remaining butter. Season to taste and stir in the parsley.
6. Chop one of the hard-boiled eggs and stir it into the mixture. Transfer to a serving dish. Slice the remaining hard-boiled egg and use to decorate the top of the kedgree.

(cont.)

MICROWAVE: this cooks well in a microwave. Place the fish in a shallow dish with the water and microwave on HIGH power for 4 minutes. Set aside. Cook the onion and half the butter in a large casserole for 4 minutes on HIGH power. Add the rice and spices to the casserole, with the fish stock, made up to 600 ml (1 pt) with *boiling* water. Microwave, uncovered, for 14 minutes, stirring once or twice. Cover and leave to stand for 5 minutes, then proceed as in steps 5 and 6.

 # BAKED MUSHROOMS

Serves 4 / Preparation: 15 minutes / Cooking: 15 minutes

These savoury stuffed mushrooms make an ideal light supper dish. Try to find large flat mushrooms, but failing that pick out the largest button mushrooms available. The filling may be varied; for a vegetarian snack substitute cheese, soaked bulgur wheat or nuts for the bacon.

8 large flat mushrooms, wiped
50 g (2 oz) butter
1 small onion, finely chopped
125 g (4 oz) smoked back bacon, rind removed and chopped
50 g (2 oz) fresh breadcrumbs
225 g (8 oz) tomatoes, chopped
15 ml (1 tbsp) chopped parsley
salt and freshly ground black pepper
butter for greasing

1. Remove the stalks from the mushrooms and reserve, then place the caps upside down in a buttered ovenproof dish.
2. Chop the mushroom stalks. Melt the butter in a frying pan and gently fry the stalks with the onion and bacon until the vegetables are soft. Stir in the remaining ingredients and remove the pan from the heat.
3. Spoon the filling into the mushroom caps, then bake in a preheated oven at 200°C (400°F), Gas Mark 6 for 15–20 minutes.

MICROWAVE: melt the butter in a bowl on HIGH power for 1 minute. Stir in the onion, bacon and chopped mushroom stalks, then cook on HIGH power for 4 minutes. Stir in the remaining ingredients then use to fill the mushroom caps. Cook on HIGH power for 4–5 minutes.

MUSHROOM STUFFED LASAGNE

Serves 4 / Preparation: 20 minutes / Cooking: 15 minutes

A delicious, nourishing dish. If you cannot get fresh pasta, use dried and follow the cooking instructions on the packet.

225 g (8 oz) fresh lasagne
15 ml (1 tbsp) oil
1 onion, finely chopped
1 clove garlic, crushed
125 g (4 oz) button mushrooms, wiped and chopped
4 tomatoes, skinned (see page 33) and chopped
25 g (1 oz) fresh breadcrumbs
salt and freshly ground black pepper
25 g (1 oz) butter
25 g (1 oz) plain flour
300 ml (½ pt) milk
25 g (1 oz) grated Parmesan cheese
butter for greasing

1. Place the lasagne in a large bowl and cover with boiling water. Leave to stand for 5 minutes.
2. Meanwhile, heat the oil in a saucepan and gently fry the onion and garlic until soft. Stir in the mushrooms and cook for 2 minutes. Remove from the heat and stir in the tomatoes, breadcrumbs and seasoning.
3. Drain the lasagne and arrange the sheets on a board. Divide the mushroom mixture equally between the sheets, then roll each one up from a short side. Arrange in a greased shallow, ovenproof dish.
4. Combine the butter, flour and milk in a saucepan and whisk over high heat until thick and smooth. Season, then pour over the filled lasagne. Sprinkle with the grated Parmesan and bake in a preheated oven at 200°C (400°F), Gas Mark 6 for 15 minutes.

MICROWAVE: soften the lasagne as in step 1. Then place the oil in a casserole with the onion and garlic. Cook on HIGH power for 2 minutes. Stir in the mushrooms and cook on HIGH power for 3 minutes. Proceed as in step 3. To make the sauce, combine the butter, flour and milk in a large jug and cook on HIGH power for 4 minutes, whisking thoroughly halfway through cooking and again on completion. Season, then pour over the lasagne and sprinkle with cheese. Cook on HIGH power for 2–3 minutes or until the cheese has melted.

QUICK PIZZA

Serves 4–6 / Preparation: 15 minutes / Cooking: 15–20 minutes

There's nothing slow about the dough used for this pizza. Based on a scone mixture, it requires no rising and bakes in under half an hour. Make two while you're about it; it freezes well.

350 g (12 oz) self-raising flour
5 ml (1 tsp) baking powder
2.5 ml (½ tsp) salt
50 g (2 oz) soft margarine
200 ml (7 fl oz) milk
oil for greasing

TOPPING
45 ml (3 tbsp) tomato purée
1 small onion, grated
2.5 ml (½ tsp) mixed dried herbs
salt and freshly ground black pepper
225 g (8 oz) grated cheese (Cheddar, Gouda or similar)
plus a selection of the following:
sliced raw mushrooms, chopped red or green pepper, sweetcorn, ham, salami,
strips of cooked chicken, chopped bacon, sliced celery, olives, anchovies,
artichoke hearts, tuna

1. Sift the flour and baking powder into a mixing bowl and add the salt. Rub in the margarine until the mixture resembles fine breadcrumbs.
2. Mix to a soft dough with the milk, adding a little more if necessary.
3. Roll out to a large rectangle or round 1 cm (½ in) thick and place on a greased baking sheet.
4. In a small bowl, mix the tomato purée, grated onion and herbs together. Spread the mixture over the pastry, leaving a clear border all round.
5. Add seasoning and additional topping ingredients as desired, and cover with the cheese. The pizza may be decorated in the traditional manner with a lattice pattern of bacon and olives.
6. Bake in a preheated ove at 200°C (400°F), Gas Mark 6 for 15–20 minutes or until crisp and golden.

CHESHIRE CHEESE TART

Serves 4 / Preparation: 10 minutes plus rising / Cooking: 20 minutes

When speed is of the essence, a bread mix is a boon. Here it forms the basis of a delicious tart which may be served with soup or salad. Vary the filling according to which cheeses you have in the refrigerator.

1 × 280 g (10 oz) packet bread mix
225g (8 oz) Cheshire cheese, grated
2 eggs, lightly beaten
150 ml (5 fl oz) single cream or top-of-the-milk
freshly ground black pepper

1. Make a bread dough, following the directions on the packet.
2. Divide the dough in half. On a lightly floured board, roll out each piece to a round about 23 cm (9 in) in diameter. Press into well greased 20 cm (8 in) flan tins or loose-bottomed cake tins, pushing the excess dough up the sides of each tin to make a base that will hold the filling in. If preferred, a single tart may be made on a flat baking sheet but the edges must again be pushed up to form a case.
3. Place the grated cheese in a bowl. Add the beaten egg and cream, stir well and season with pepper.
4. Divide the filling between the tarts and leave to rise in a warm place for 15 minutes.
5. Bake in a preheated oven at 220°C (425°F), Gas Mark 7 for 20 minutes or until golden brown. Cut each tart in half to serve.

CURRY PASTIES

Serves 4 / Preparation: 20 minutes plus cooling /
Cooking: 20 minutes

Pasties make the perfect finger food. These have a lovely moist filling. Make them smaller than suggested to serve with drinks. They may be frozen uncooked or after they have been baked.

15 ml (1 tbsp) oil
1 onion, finely chopped
225 g (8 oz) lean minced beef
5 ml (1 tsp) curry powder
5 ml (1 tsp) tomato purée
30 ml (2 tbsp) mango chutney
salt and freshly ground black pepper
a little milk for glazing

SHORTCRUST PASTRY
350 g (12 oz) plain flour
2.5 ml (½ tsp) salt
75 g (3 oz) margarine
75 g (3 oz) lard
60 ml (4 tbsp) water

1. Heat the oil in a saucepan, add the onion and fry gently until beginning to soften.
2. Stir in the beef and fry until browned, then stir in the curry powder. Cook for 2 minutes more.
3. Add the tomato purée and chutney. Stir well, breaking up any large pieces of mango. Add a little water if necessary; the mixture should be fairly dry. Season to taste and set aside to cool.
4. Make the pastry. Sift the flour and salt into a mixing bowl. Rub in the margarine and lard until the mixture resembles fine breadcrumbs. Stir in the water, then knead together lightly to form a smooth dough.
5. On a floured board, roll out the dough and cut out eight 13 cm (5 in) circles, using a saucer as a guide, if liked.
6. Divide the mince mixture between the pasty rounds, then fold in half, moistening one edge lightly with water to seal. Crimp the edges of each pasty. Place on a baking sheet and brush with the milk.
7. Bake in a preheated oven at 190°C (375°F), Gas Mark 5 for 20 minutes or until golden.

MICROWAVE: combine the oil and onion in a bowl and cook on HIGH power for 4 minutes. Stir in the meat and curry powder and cook for 4 minutes on HIGH power, then add the tomato purée and chutney. Stir and cook for a further 5 minutes on HIGH power. Season and cool. Proceed from step 5, baking the pasties in a conventional oven.

GRILLED SOLE AND BACON ROLLS

Serves 2 / Preparation: 10 minutes / Cooking: 6 minutes

The combination of bacon and fish in this simple dish is unusual and delicious. It may be prepared in advance and cooked at the last minute.

1 large sole, filleted and skinned
4 large broad rashers streaky bacon, rinds removed
freshly ground black pepper
15 ml (1 tbsp) lemon juice
50 g (2 oz) Cheddar cheese, grated
butter for greasing

1. Wash the fish if necessary and pat dry with absorbent kitchen paper. Use the back of a knife to stretch each bacon rasher.
2. Lay a fillet of sole on top of each rasher, season with pepper and roll up.
3. Arrange the rolls in a greased shallow flameproof dish and sprinkle with the lemon juice and cheese. Cook under a preheated medium grill for about 6 minutes or until the fish flakes easily when tested with the tip of a knife, and the bacon is brown.
4. Serve immediately with granary bread to mop up the juices.

MICROWAVE: follow steps 1 to 3 but cook, covered in the microwave on HIGH power for 4 minutes.

TUNA AND BEAN SALAD

Serves 2–4 / Preparation: 5 minutes plus optional standing time

'Here's a starter for four.' Not an introduction to a quiz show, but a high-fibre salad that's certain to bring you top marks from family and friends.

1 × 198 g (7 oz) can tuna in water or brine, drained
1 × 400g (14 oz) can white kidney beans, borlotti beans, haricot beans or
black-eyed beans, drained

1 onion, finely chopped
1 clove garlic, crushed (optional)
30 ml (2 tbsp) lemon juice
salt and plenty of freshly ground black pepper
lettuce leaves

1. Break the tuna into large flakes and place it in a bowl. Rinse the beans gently under cold water, drain thoroughly and add to the bowl.
2. Add all the remaining ingredients except the lettuce, seasoning to taste.
3. Cover the bowl and set aside for an hour or so if you have time so that the flavours may mingle. Serve piled on lettuce.

HOT CHICKEN SALAD

Serves 2 / Preparation and Cooking: 20 minutes

A wide variety of salad ingredients are now finding their way into our shops. This recipe uses some of the leaves. Use at least two types, preferably of different colours.

A selection of salad leaves
(e.g. Iceberg lettuce, frissé, radicchio, chicory, red cabbage, lollo rosso, watercress)
45 ml (3 tbsp) Vinaigrette (page 94)
1 boneless chicken breast, skinned
25 g (1 oz) butter
2 rashers smoked streaky bacon, rind removed and diced
30 ml (2 tbsp) sunflower oil
1 slice stale bread, in small cubes
30 ml (2 tbsp) mayonnaise (optional)

1. Wash and dry the salad leaves and arrange either on two plates or in a serving bowl. Add the vinaigrette and toss lightly.
2. Cut the chicken breast into thin strips. Heat the butter in a frying pan, add the chicken and fry quickly until it is brown on all sides and cooked through. Remove from the pan with a slotted spoon and keep warm.
3. Add the bacon to the fat remaining in the pan and fry until crisp. Remove with a slotted spoon and add to the chicken. Keep warm.
4. Add the oil to the frying pan. When it is hot, cook the bread cubes until golden brown and crisp.
5. Pile the chicken, bacon and bread croutons on to the salad, top with the mayonnaise if using and serve immediately.

CONTINENTAL BEAN FEAST

Serves 4 / Preparation: 15 minutes / Cooking: 5 minutes

This is a salad to beat all, brimming with texture and flavour. Serve it with lots of garlic bread and Wimbledon-watching will never be the same again.

450 g (1 lb) frozen French beans
30 ml (2 tbsp) olive oil
1 small onion, finely chopped
1 clove garlic, crushed
15 ml (1 tbsp) wine vinegar
salt and freshly ground black pepper
450 g (1 lb) tomatoes, sliced
125 g (4 oz) salami bought in one piece, then skinned and roughly chopped
175 g (6 oz) Feta or Cheshire cheese, cubed
a handful of black olives

1. Preheat the grill.
2. Plunge the beans into a saucepan of boiling water. Boil for 2 minutes. Drain, plunge into iced water to refresh the beans, then drain again. Cut into 2.5 cm (1 in) lengths and set aside.
3. Heat the oil in a saucepan and gently fry the onion and garlic until soft. Remove from the heat, then stir in the wine vinegar and seasoning.
4. Stir in the beans with the tomatoes and salami, then pour into a shallow flameproof dish. Sprinkle the cheese over the top.
5. Flash under the hot grill until the cheese begins to brown. Serve immediately, sprinkled with the black olives.

MICROWAVE: place the frozen beans in a casserole, cover and cook on HIGH power for 6 minutes, stirring occasionally. Leave to cool, then cut into 2.5 cm (1 in) lengths. Place the oil in a shallow dish and stir in the onion and garlic. Cook on HIGH power for 3 minutes, then stir in the wine vinegar, beans, tomatoes and salami. Sprinkle over the cheese. Heat in the microwave on HIGH power for 4–5 minutes or until heated through.

LEEK AND BACON ROLLS AU GRATIN

Serves 4 / Preparation: 5 minutes / Cooking: 35 minutes

Serve this light supper dish with chunks of wholemeal bread. Choose tender young leeks and a good smoked bacon for the best results. For a crisper topping a few wholemeal breadcrumbs could be mixed with the cheese.

8 leeks
salt and freshly ground black pepper
8 rashers smoked streaky bacon, rinds removed
25 g (1 oz) margarine
25 g (1 oz) plain flour
300 ml (½ pt) milk
50 g (2 oz) Cheddar cheese, grated

1. Trim the leeks, leaving them whole. Wash thoroughly, then plunge into a large saucepan of boiling, salted water. Cover and cook for 6–8 minutes or until just tender.
2. Drain the leeks thoroughly. Wrap a rasher of bacon spiral-fashion around each leek. Arrange in a shallow, ovenproof dish.
3. Combine the margarine, flour and milk in a saucepan and bring to the boil, whisking constantly. Boil for 1 minute, stirring until thick and smooth. Season, then pour over the leeks.
4. Sprinkle with cheese and bake in a preheated oven at 190°C (375°), Gas Mark 5 for 25–30 minutes.

MICROWAVE: place the cleaned and trimmed leeks in a single layer in a shallow dish. Add 45 ml (3 tbsp) water, cover and cook on HIGH power for 6 minutes. Drain, wrap in bacon and return to the dish. Combine the margarine, flour and milk in a large jug and cook on HIGH power for 4 minutes, whisking thoroughly halfway through cooking and again on completion. Season, then pour over the leeks. Sprinkle with cheese and cook on MEDIUM power for 12–15 minutes or until the bacon is tender.

MAIN
FEATURES

Whatever your budget, you will find a main feature here that is certain to please family and friends. The recipes are not epic, and you won't need to do battle with the ingredients, but they may well become classics in your repertoire! We give a new slant to tried and tested old timers such as Steak and kidney in golden boxes and Crispy-topped pork chops, and welcome promising newcomers such as Chicken and bacon gougere. The accent throughout is on healthy meals prepared with the minimum of fuss.

GOUJONS OF PLAICE IN OATMEAL

Serves 4 / Preparation: 15 minutes / Cooking: 10 minutes

Herrings in oatmeal are a traditional Scottish breakfast dish, and this is a quick variation on the same theme. You could try them while watching breakfast TV, but we think them more appropriate for a TV supper! Serve them with sauce tartare. They may be frozen uncooked provided fresh plaice has been used for the goujons.

450 g (1 lb) plaice fillets, skinned
125 g (4 oz) medium oatmeal
salt and freshly ground black pepper
60 ml (4 tbsp) oil

1. Cut the fish into strips, approximately 1 × 4 cm (½ × 1½ in).
2. Put the oatmeal in a plastic bag with a little salt and pepper, add the fish and shake to coat evenly. Remove from bag and shake off excess oatmeal.
3. Heat the oil in a large frying pan. Add the goujons, a few at a time, and cook over moderate heat until golden brown. Drain on absorbent kitchen paper and serve at once.

PRAWN CREOLE

Serves 2–3 / Preparation: 10 minutes / Cooking: 10 minutes

Serve this with plain boiled rice for a fork supper that's as easy to prepare as it is to eat. There is no need to use fresh shellfish; the less costly frozen prawns are ideal for a dish such as this.

25 g (1 oz) butter
2 cloves garlic, crushed
1 onion, finely chopped
150 ml (¼ pt) dry white wine
4 tomatoes, skinned (see page 33) and chopped
15 ml (1 tbsp) tomato purée
5 ml (1 tsp) ground mace
10 ml (2 tsp) cornflour
30 ml (2 tbsp) water
225 g (8 oz) cooked, peeled prawns, thawed if frozen
salt and freshly ground black pepper

1. Melt the butter in a saucepan and stir in the garlic and onion. Cook gently until soft. Add the wine, tomatoes, tomato purée and mace and bring to the boil.
2. Meanwhile blend the cornflour with the water in a cup. Stir into the tomato mixture. Return to the boil, stirring constantly.
3. Stir in the prawns and heat through over low heat. Season to taste.

MICROWAVE: melt the butter in a casserole on HIGH power for 1 minute. Stir in the garlic and onion and cook on HIGH power for 2 minutes. Stir in the wine, tomatoes, tomato purée and mace, cover and cook on HIGH power for 4 minutes. Blend the cornflour with the water and stir in with the prawns. Cook on HIGH power for 3–4 minutes or until thoroughly heated through. Stir occasionally.

FISHERMAN'S PIE

Serves 2 / Preparation: 10 minutes / Cooking: 30 minutes

Using convenience foods — frozen fish in sauce, and frozen pastry — cuts preparation time to the absolute minimum. Make this in individual parcels if you prefer, dividing the pastry in half and rolling each portion to a rectangle large enough to encase a block of frozen fish in sauce. Bring each corner into the centre and seal well before baking (see illustration below right). Freeze uncooked, if desired.

225 g (8 oz) frozen puff pastry, thawed
2 × 170 g (6 oz) packets frozen cod in parsley sauce or butter sauce
50 g (2 oz) frozen peas
1 egg, beaten, to glaze

1. On a floured board, roll out the pastry to a 35 × 30 cm (14 × 12 in) rectangle. Trim the edges, reserving the trimmings.
2. Remove each block of frozen fish from its wrappings and place in the centre of the pastry. Cover with the peas.
3. Fold in the top and bottom edges of the pastry as shown in the sketch (below left), sealing with the egg. Transfer to a baking sheet.
4. Roll out the trimmings and cut into fish shapes. Use these to decorate the top of the pie, keeping them in place with a dab of beaten egg.
5. Finally brush the pie with more beaten egg, and bake in a preheated oven at 200°C (400°F), Gas Mark 6 for 30 minutes, or until the pie is well risen and golden.

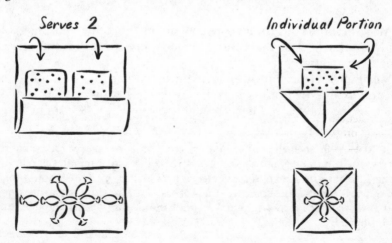

Serves 2   Individual Portion

COD AND PEPPER PACKETS

Serves 4 / Preparation: 15 minutes / Cooking: 20 minutes

Some people avoid cooking fish because of the smell. In this recipe the problem doesn't arise, as the fish is cooked in neat little foil parcels which contain all the flavour, juices and aroma. This is a light but flavoursome dish which is also low in calories.

4 × 175 g (6 oz) cod or haddock cutlets
1 large green pepper, cored, seeded and sliced
1 onion, thinly sliced
4 tomatoes, skinned (see page 33) and roughly chopped
125 g (4 oz) button mushrooms, wiped and sliced
30 ml (2 tbsp) lemon juice
50 g (2 oz) black olives, stoned
2.5 ml (½ tsp) mixed dried herbs
salt and freshly ground black pepper
125 g (4 oz) Edam cheese, grated

1. Wipe the fish, then place each cutlet on a piece of foil large enough to contain it.
2. Combine the green pepper, onion, tomatoes, mushrooms and lemon juice in a saucepan, cover and cook over gentle heat for 5 minutes, shaking the pan occasionally.
3. Stir in the olives and herbs and adjust the seasoning. Spoon a quarter of the mixture over the top of each cutlet. Sprinkle over the cheese.
4. Bring up the foil to form four loose parcels. Place these in a roasting tin and cook in a preheated oven at 180°C (350°F), Gas Mark 4 for 20 minutes or until the fish flakes easily when tested with the tip of a knife.

MICROWAVE: place the fish on pieces of greaseproof paper instead of the foil. Combine the green pepper, onion, tomatoes, mushrooms and lemon juice in a dish, cover and cook on HIGH power for 3 minutes. Follow the wrapping instructions in steps 4 and 5, placing the parcels in a suitable shallow dish. Cook on HIGH power for 5–7 minutes. Test as above.

NORTH SEA COBBLER

Serves 4 / Preparation: 15 minutes / Cooking: 20 minutes

This is a fish pie with a difference. The cheesy scone topping makes a welcome change from potato or pastry and as the cobbler includes fresh vegetables it makes an ideal one-dish meal. We have used boil-in-the-bag fish for convenience, but obviously fresh, poached fish and a sauce could be used instead. Vary the vegetables according to season, but always use a fast cooking variety. Freeze after topping with scone dough, but before baking. Frozen peas or a can of sweetcorn could be substituted for the courgettes.

4 × 170 g (6 oz) packets frozen cod steaks in butter sauce
15 g (½ oz) butter
225 g (8 oz) courgettes, thinly sliced
milk, to glaze

TOPPING
225 g (8 oz) self-raising flour
50 g (2 oz) margarine
50 g (2 oz) Cheddar cheese, grated
150 ml (¼ pt) milk

1. Cook the cod according to the instruction on the packet.
2. Melt the butter in a large saucepan and gently fry the courgettes until slightly softened.
3. Slit the bags and transfer the fish and sauce to an 18 cm (7 in) soufflé dish or casserole. Flake the fish with a fork, then stir the courgettes into the mixture.
4. To make the topping, sift the flour into a mixing bowl and rub in the margarine until the mixture resembles fine breadcrumbs. Add the cheese, then stir in the milk. Knead together lightly to form a soft dough.
5. Roll out the dough on a floured surface to an 18 cm (7 in) round, then cut into 8 wedges. Arrange the wedges on top of the fish, brush with milk and bake in a preheated oven at 200°C (400°F), Gas Mark 6 for 20 minutes or until golden brown.

MICROWAVE: the cod may be cooked in the microwave, following the instructions on the packet. Combine the courgettes and the butter in a bowl, cover and cook on HIGH power for 5 minutes. Proceed as in steps 3 to 5, baking the completed cobbler in a conventional oven.

PASTA WITH TUNA AND PEAS

Serves 2 / Preparation: 5 minutes / Cooking: 20 minutes

This is a good store cupboard standby, quickly made and very tasty. Any pasta shapes may be used; spirals or bows look attractive, but shells would keep the seafood theme.

15 ml (1 tbsp) oil
175 g (6 oz) pasta shapes
1 × 200 g (7 oz) can tuna in brine or water
25 g (1 oz) butter
25 g (1 oz) plain flour
150 ml (¼ pt) milk
125 g (4 oz) frozen petit pois
salt and freshly ground black pepper to taste

1. Bring a large saucepan of salted water to the boil. Add the oil and pasta, return to the boil, then cover the pan and remove from the heat. Leave to stand for 10–12 minutes or until cooked but still firm to the bite.
2. Meanwhile drain the tuna, reserving the liquid from the can. Flake the fish and set aside.
3. Melt the butter in a saucepan, add the flour and cook for 1 minute. Remove from the heat and gradually stir in the milk and the liquid drained from the tuna, whisking constantly until smooth.
4. Return to the heat and bring to the boil, stirring constantly until the sauce thickens. Add the peas and cook for 2 minutes, then stir in the flaked fish, with seasoning to taste. Thin if necessary with a little extra milk.
5. Drain the pasta, transfer to a serving dish and stir in the sauce. Serve immediately.

MICROWAVE: the pasta is best cooked on the hob. Make the sauce by combining the butter, flour and liquid in a large jug. Cook on HIGH power for 4 minutes, whisking frequently. Add the peas and cook for 2 minutes more on HIGH power. Add fish and seasoning. Proceed as in step 5.

CURRIED HADDOCK

Serves 4 / Preparation and Cooking: 20 minutes

Most curries need long slow simmering to achieve their potential; this curried fish dish is quickly cooked to ensure that both the texture and the essential flavour of the fish is maintained, and it is enhanced, not overwhelmed by the subtle curry sauce. Serve it with rice and a simple chopped tomato and onion salad, dressed with lemon juice and a little sugar, and sprinkled with chopped coriander. Any firm white fish may be used, but it should be fresh. If you must use frozen, reduce the quantity of stock to 300 ml (½ pt).

25 g (1 oz) butter
1 clove garlic, crushed
1 onion, chopped
15 ml (1 tbsp) plain flour
15 ml (1 tbsp) mild curry powder or paste
grated rind and juice of ½ lemon
450 ml (¾ pt) chicken stock
10 ml (2 tsp) tomato purée
30 ml (2 tbsp) sweet chutney
25 g (1 oz) sultanas
450 g (1 lb) haddock, skinned and cubed
cooked rice to serve

1. Melt the butter in a large saucepan and add the garlic and onion. Cook gently until the vegetables begin to soften.
2. Stir in the flour and curry powder and cook for 2 minutes. Remove from the heat and gradually stir in the rind and lemon juice and the chicken stock.
3. Bring to the boil, stirring constantly, and stir in all the remaining ingredients. Lower the heat, cover and simmer gently for 5 minutes or until the fish is cooked, stirring occasionally. Serve with rice.

MICROWAVE: this cooks well in the microwave. Use a large bowl and cook the butter, garlic and onion on HIGH power for 4 minutes. Then stir in the flour and curry powder and cook on HIGH power for 1 minute more. Gradually stir in the liquid and cook on HIGH power for 4 minutes. Finally add all the remaining ingredients, cover and cook on HIGH power for 5 minutes.

CHEESY FISH PARCELS

Serves 4 / Preparation: 10 minutes / Cooking: 20 minutes

Whatever the occasion – a simple Sunday night supper; a late lunch while you catch up on your favourite sporting fixture – good things come in small parcels. Serve solo, with salad or with a colourful vegetable stir-fry. If the fish is dried well you should be able to prepare this in advance without it spoiling, provided it is kept cool. The prepared parcels may be frozen uncooked provided fresh fish was used for the filling.

350 g (12 oz) frozen puff pastry, thawed
450 g (1 lb) smoked haddock or smoked cod
125 g (4 oz) mushrooms, wiped and sliced
125 g (4 oz) Edam cheese, sliced
freshly ground black pepper
1 egg, beaten, to glaze

1. On a floured board, roll out the pastry to a thickness of 5 mm (¼ in). Trim the edges and divide into 4 equal squares.
2. Pat the fish dry with absorbent kitchen paper, then divide into four. Place a piece of fish on each pastry square and top each with a quarter of the mushrooms and 25 g (1 oz) of the cheese. Season with pepper.
3. Dampen the edges of the pastry and fold over the top and bottom as shown in the illustrations for Fisherman's pie (page 48) pressing the edges to seal them firmly.
4. Brush each parcel with beaten egg, place on a baking sheet and cook in a preheated oven at 200°C (400°F), Gas Mark 6 for 15–20 minutes or until well risen and golden brown.

TIP: use filo pastry for an even easier parcel – there is no need to roll it out but brush with plenty of melted butter.

SAUSAGE STEW

Serves 4 / Preparation: 10 minutes / Cooking: 35 minutes

Serve this speedy stew with buttered noodles or jacket potatoes to make a cheap but hearty supper. We often use herby sausages which give a good flavour, and sometimes add potatoes to make a dish that needs no further accompaniment.

15 ml (1 tbsp) oil
450 g (1 lb) thick pork sausages
1 onion, sliced
3 sticks celery, sliced
2 carrots, scraped and cut into matchsticks
1 × 400 g (14 oz) can tomatoes
150 ml (¼ pt) chicken stock
salt and freshly ground black pepper

1. Heat the oil in a large saucepan and quickly brown the sausages. Stir in the onion, celery and carrots and cook for 2 minutes, stirring constantly.
2. Add the tomatoes, with their juices. Stir in the stock, bring to the boil, then lower the heat, cover and simmer for 25–30 minutes. Season to taste before serving.

MICROWAVE: the sausages must be browned quickly. This could be done in a browning dish. Add the vegetables and cook on HIGH power for 2 minutes. Stir in the remaining ingredients and cook on HIGH power for 5 minutes then on MEDIUM power for 25–30 minutes or until the vegetables are tender.

SAUSAGE PLAIT

Serves 4 / Preparation: 15 minutes / Cooking: 30 minutes

Sausage rolls can be disappointing because there is often more roll than sausage. This is a much tastier alternative, which may be varied according to the contents of your freezer or refrigerator. Try adding a little bacon or sliced mushrooms. Freeze the plait after baking.

225 g (8 oz) pork sausagemeat
1 onion, grated
50 g (2 oz) fresh white breadcrumbs
30 ml (2 tbsp) pickle
2.5 ml (½ tsp) mixed dried herbs
salt and freshly ground black pepper
1 egg, beaten
1 × 215 g (7½ oz) packet frozen puff pastry, thawed

1. In a large bowl, combine the sausagemeat, onion, breadcrumbs, pickle and herbs. Add seasoning to taste, mix well and add half the egg.
2. On a floured board, roll out the pastry to a rectangle 35 × 30 cm (14 × 12 in).
3. Put the sausage mixture down the centre of the pastry, leaving 2.5 cm (1 in) clear at the top and bottom.
4. Using a sharp knife, cut diagonal strips every 2.5 cm (1 in) down each side of the pastry, stopping just short of the filling. Brush the edges with a little of the remaining beaten egg.

5. Fold in the top and bottom and plait alternate strips of pastry over the filling. Place on a baking sheet.
6. Brush the plait generously with the remaining egg and bake in a preheated oven at 190°C (375°F), Gas Mark 5 for 30 minutes or until well risen and golden.

BAVARIAN SAUSAGE RAGOÛT

Serves 4 / Preparation: 15 minutes / Cooking: 15 minutes

The German-style sausages which are now readily available are a really useful addition to the store cupboard. (Many of them need not be kept in the refrigerator until opened.) They may be eaten hot or cold and can be used in a wide variety of dishes. Try them sliced in the German pea soup on page 19 or enjoy them in this colourful one-pan meal.

50 g (2 oz) butter or margarine
1 large onion, chopped
1 large red pepper, cored, seeded and chopped
450 g (1 lb) courgettes, sliced
15 ml (1 tbsp) plain flour
600 ml (1 pt) milk
4 tomatoes, skinned (see page 33) and roughly chopped
225 g (8 oz) smoked pork sausage, sliced
salt and freshly ground black pepper

1. Melt the butter in a large saucepan and gently fry the onion and pepper until soft. Stir in the courgettes, cover and sweat over a gentle heat for 10 minutes, shaking the pan occasionally.
2. Stir in the flour and cook for 1 minute. Gradually stir in the milk, then bring to the boil, stirring constantly.
3. Add the tomatoes and sausage, stir gently, then lower the heat, cover and simmer for 5–10 minutes or until the vegetables are tender. Season to taste, then serve.

MICROWAVE: melt the butter in a casserole on HIGH power for 1½ minutes. Stir in the onion and pepper, cover and cook on HIGH power for 4 minutes. Stir in the courgettes, cover and cook on HIGH power for 6 minutes, stirring occasionally. Mix in the flour, then gradually blend in the milk. Cover and cook on HIGH power for 8–10 minutes or until thickened, stirring occasionally. Finally stir in the tomatoes and sausage, cover and cook on HIGH power for 4–5 minutes, stirring halfway through cooking. Season to taste.

CRISPY-TOPPED PORK CHOPS

Serves 4 / Preparation: 10 minutes / Cooking: 15–20 minutes

Here is a simple way of serving that time-honoured combination, pork and apple. If time permits, fry the chops instead of grilling them, then use the juices to make a sauce by adding 45 ml (3 tbsp) cider or white wine and 150 ml (¼ pt) double cream. Boil until slightly thickened, then season and serve with the chops.

4 pork chops
1 eating apple, cored and chopped
125 g (4 oz) Gouda cheese, grated
15 ml (1 tbsp) cream or top-of-the-milk
freshly ground black pepper

1. Place the chops under a preheated grill until cooked through, turning over halfway through the cooking time. Cooking time will be between 12 and 16 minutes, depending on the size and thickness of the chops.
2. Mix all the remaining ingredients in a bowl. Spoon on top of the chops. Return to the grill and cook until the cheese has melted.

STEAK AND KIDNEY IN GOLDEN BOXES

Serves 6 / Preparation: 20 minutes / Cooking: 2½ hours

A new way with a old favourite, but much easier to serve. If the steak and kidney is made in advance you will simply have to bake the boxes.

30 ml (2 tbsp) sunflower oil
1 large onion, sliced
675 g (1½ lb) steak and kidney
25 g (1 oz) plain flour
salt and freshly ground black pepper to taste
300 ml (½ pt) beef stock, or half stock and half wine
15 ml (1 tbsp) tomato purée
2.5 ml (½ tsp) mixed dried herbs

BOXES
450 g (1 lb) frozen puff pastry, thawed
beaten egg to glaze

1. Heat the oil in a saucepan and sauté the onion until soft.
2. Cut up the steak and kidney if necessary into 2.5 cm (1 in) cubes. Place the flour in a plastic bag with seasoning, add the steak and kidney and toss until well coated.
3. Add the floured meat to the onions and fry until browned all over, then stir in any remaining flour.
4. Gradually add the liquid, stirring constantly. Stir in the tomato purée and the herbs and bring to the boil.
5. Either cover and simmer gently on the hob or transfer to a casserole, cover and cook in a preheated oven at 160°C (325°F), Gas Mark 3 for about 1½–2 hours or until the meat is tender. If this is cooked in the oven it will need stirring once; check more often if it is being cooked on the hob. Season to taste when the meat is tender.
6. On a floured board, roll out the pastry to a large rectangle 1 cm (½ in) thick. Cut out six 15 × 10 cm (6 × 4 in) rectangles. It may be easier to use only half the pastry at a time, cutting three boxes from each piece. Place the rectangles on baking sheets.
7. Without cutting all the way through the pastry, score a line 1 cm (½ in) inside each box. Score the central area in a criss-cross pattern (see illustration opposite). Brush well with beaten egg.

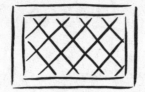

8. Bake the boxes in a preheated oven at 220°C (425°F), Gas Mark 7 for 10–15 minutes or until golden.
9. Carefully lift out the scored central lid of pastry from each box, fill the cavities with steak and kidney, replace the lids and serve immediately.

KIDNEY KEBABS

Serves 4 / Preparation: 10 minutes / Cooking: 10 minutes

This is a good way to cook kidneys which requires no additional fat, thanks to the woven bacon jacket. Serve it with rice or creamed potatoes and gravy.

8 lambs' kidneys
4 rashers streaky bacon

1. Cut each kidney in quarters. Remove the rind from the bacon and stretch each rasher slightly with the back of a knife.
2. Thread the end of a bacon rasher on to a skewer. Follow with a piece of kidney, then pierce the bacon again with the skewer. Repeat until eight pieces of kidney have been interwoven with bacon on the skewer (see illustration below).
3. Cook under a preheated hot grill, turning once or twice, for about 10 minutes. Serve immediately.

MICROWAVE: this cooks perfectly in the microwave. It will take 8 minutes on HIGH power, turning once. Use wooden skewers, arranging them in a square with the centre free. Cover to cook.

LIVER AND BACON LAYER

Serves 4 / Preparation: 15 minutes / Cooking: 30–35 minutes

If your opinion of liver is coloured by memories of meals where the main ingredient was tough and unpalatable, do try this simply delicious dish in which tender liver is complemented by a savoury stuffing. Sage is a highly compatible herb. The Italians fry liver swiftly in butter with fresh sage for a taste that is sensational. Try it and see, but be sure to use lamb's or calf's liver for the most tender results.

450 g (1 lb) lamb's liver
125 g (4 oz) fresh white breadcrumbs
15 ml (1 tbsp) chopped parsley
5 ml (1 tsp) dried sage
1 onion, finely chopped
salt and freshly ground black pepper
300 ml (½ pt) hot beef stock
6 rashers smoked back bacon, rind removed

1. Slice the liver thinly, discarding any membrane or gristle, then place half in the base of a 20 cm (8 in) casserole.
2. Mix the breadcrumbs, parsley, sage, onion and seasoning in a bowl. Spread half of this mixture over the liver. Repeat with the remaining liver and breadcrumbs.
3. Pour over the stock, then cover the surface of the mixture with the rashers of bacon. Cook in a preheated oven at 190°C (375°F), Gas Mark 5 for 30–35 minutes or until the bacon is crisp and the liver tender.

✳ CASSEROLE OF POTATO AND BACON

Serves 4 / Preparation: 15 minutes / Cooking: 40–50 minutes

This is a warming winter supper dish. Slice the potatoes as thinly as possible to speed up the cooking time, using a food processor or the slicing edge of a hand grater. Add a salad or fresh green vegetable for a well-balanced meal.

675 g (1½ lb) potatoes, peeled and thinly sliced
225 g (8 oz) smoked streaky bacon, rind removed, chopped
1 small onion, finely chopped
15 ml (1 tbsp) chopped parsley
salt and freshly ground black pepper
175 g (6 oz) Cheddar cheese, grated
10 ml (2 tsp) cornflour
300 ml (½ pt) hot chicken stock
butter for greasing

1. Layer the potatoes with the bacon, onion, parsley, seasoning and cheese in a buttered casserole.
2. Blend the cornflour with a little water in a cup, then combine with the stock in a measuring jug. Pour into the casserole.
3. Bake in a preheated oven at 200°C (400°F), Gas Mark 6 for 40–50 minutes or until the potatoes are tender.

MICROWAVE: follow steps 1 and 2, but cook in the microwave on HIGH power for 25–30 minutes or until the potato is tender.

SUNNY SPICE EGGS

Serves 4 / Preparation: 20 minutes / Cooking: 20 minutes

This has a wonderful yellow colour which contrasts well with the green of the spinach. It tastes mild yet rich. Creamed coconut is available in large supermarkets and Indian grocers; it is a useful addition to curries. If unobtainable, a suitable substitute may be made by soaking 125 g (4 oz) unsweetened desiccated coconut in 450 ml (¾ pt) milk, then straining the milk, discarding the solids.

125 g (4 oz) creamed coconut
15 ml (1 tbsp) oil
1 large onion, chopped
1 clove garlic, crushed
2 tomatoes, chopped
5 ml (1 tsp) turmeric
2.5 ml (½ tsp) chilli powder
salt and freshly ground black pepper to taste
25 g (1 oz) butter
350 g (12 oz) cooked chopped spinach, drained
4 eggs

1. Cut the creamed coconut into cubes and place in a measuring jug. Make up to 450 ml (¾ pt) with boiling water. Set aside.
2. Heat the oil in a saucepan and fry the onion and garlic until soft. Add the chopped tomatoes, turmeric and chilli and cook for 2 minutes.
3. Add the coconut mixture and simmer for 5 minutes. Purée in a blender or food processor or push through a sieve into a bowl. Season to taste.
4. Use the butter to generously grease a gratin dish. Season the spinach, then spread on the base. Using the back of a spoon, make four hollows in the spinach. Crack an egg into each, then pour the sauce over the top.
5. Bake in a preheated oven at 180°C (350°F), Gas Mark 4 for 20–25 minutes or until the eggs are just firm. Serve at once.

SWEET AND SOUR GAMMON

Serves 6 / Preparation: 20 minutes / Cooking: 15 minutes

Ever get the feeling you're watching a repeat when you view your post-Christmas table? There's a limit to the amount of cold turkey and ham anyone can consume, so give the leftovers the Oriental touch with this tasty supper dish.

30 ml (2 tbsp) oil
225 g (8 oz) onions, roughly chopped
1 garlic clove, crushed
125 g (4 oz) carrots, scraped and cut into sticks
125 g (4 oz) green pepper, cored, seeded and cut into rings
75 g (3 oz) button mushrooms, wiped and sliced
5 ml (1 tsp) grated fresh ginger
1 × 200 g (7 oz) can pineapple chunks in natural juice
15 ml (1 tbsp) red wine vinegar
15 ml (1 tbsp) tomato purée
30 ml (2 tbsp) soy sauce
15 ml (1 tbsp) soft light brown sugar
15 ml (1 tbsp) cornflour
75 g (3 oz) canned water chestnuts, drained and sliced
350 g (12 oz) cooked gammon, ham or turkey, diced

1. Heat the oil in a saucepan and fry the onions, garlic and carrots until beginning to soften. Stir in the pepper, mushrooms and ginger and cook for 1 minute.
2. Drain the pineapple, reserving the juice in a measuring jug. Set the pineapple chunks aside and make up the juice to 350 ml (12 fl oz) with water. Stir in the vinegar, tomato purée, soy sauce and sugar.
3. Pour a little of the liquid from the measuring jug into a cup, add the cornflour and mix to a smooth paste. Add to the remaining pineapple juice mixture, then stir into the vegetables. Bring to the boil, stirring constantly and then add the water chestnuts, gammon and reserved pineapple chunks.
4. Cook for about 4 minutes, stirring occasionally, until heated through. Serve with rice or noodles.

MICROWAVE: cook the vegetables with the oil in a large bowl on HIGH power for 6 minutes, stirring once or twice. Follow steps 2 and 3, adding the cornflour and pineapple juice mixture to the vegetables. Cook on HIGH power for 6 minutes, stirring twice, or until the sauce is boiling. Add all the remaining ingredients and cook on HIGH power for 4 minutes or until hot.

CHILLI CON CARNE

Serves 4 / Preparation: 15 minutes / Cooking: 1 hour

This is our favourite recipe for Chilli; easy to make and packed with flavour – and fibre! It freezes well so it is worth making a large quantity and freezing some to serve solo or as a topping for baked jacket potatoes.

30 ml (2 tbsp) oil
1 onion, chopped
1 clove garlic, crushed
450 g (1 lb) lean minced beef
125 g (4 oz) green pepper, cored, seeded and chopped
10 ml (2 tsp) chilli powder
5 ml (1 tsp) paprika
5 ml (1 tsp) cumin
10 ml (2 tsp) plain flour
2.5 ml (½ tsp) salt
1 × 400 g (14 oz) can chopped tomatoes
10 ml (2 tsp) tomato purée
300 ml (½ pt) water
1 × 400 g (14 oz) can red kidney beans, drained, rinsed and drained again

1. Heat the oil in a large saucepan and fry the onion and garlic until soft. Add the minced beef, breaking it up well with a wooden spoon.
2. When the meat has browned add the green pepper, chilli powder, paprika, cumin, flour and salt. Stir well and cook for a further 4 minutes.
3. Stir in the tomatoes, the tomato purée and the water. Lower the heat, cover and simmer for 45 minutes.
4. Add the beans and simmer for 15 minutes more.

MICROWAVE: this may be cooked in a large bowl in the microwave. Allow 4 minutes on HIGH power for the onions and garlic to cook with the oil. Add the meat and cook for 4 minutes on HIGH power, stirring twice, then add the green pepper and dry ingredients and cook for 4 minutes on HIGH power. Follow step 3, but cook for 10 minutes on HIGH power, then 20 minutes on MEDIUM power. Finally add the beans and cook for a further 10 minutes on MEDIUM power. For the best flavour leave to stand overnight, then reheat.

TIP: to make an economical curried mince, omit the spices, tomatoes and beans and replace with 10 ml (2 tsp) of curry powder or paste. A delicious dish that improves with standing.

BOLOGNESE SAUCE

Serves 4 / Preparation: 15 minutes / Cooking: 20 minutes

This is a really useful recipe with endless variations. Beyond the obvious Spaghetti Bolognese, it can form the basis of a shepherd's pie, lasagne, pancake filling or the soft centre of a pie or pasty. It is a good idea to make up three or four times the quantity and freeze in usable portions.

15 ml (1 tbsp) oil
1 onion, finely chopped
1 clove garlic, crushed
5 ml (1 tsp) dried mixed herbs
1 carrot, scraped and finely chopped
125 g (4 oz) button mushrooms, wiped and sliced
450 g (1 lb) minced beef
15 ml (1 tbsp) plain flour
1 × 400 g (14 oz) can chopped tomatoes
30 ml (2 tbsp) tomato purée
150 ml (¼ pt) beef stock
salt and freshly ground black pepper

1. Heat the oil in a saucepan and gently fry the onion and garlic until soft.
2. Stir in the herbs, carrot, mushrooms and minced beef and cook gently until the meat is browned, stirring frequently.
3. Stir in the flour and cook for 1 minute, lower the heat, then stir in the remaining ingredients. Bring to the boil, then cover, lower the heat and simmer gently for 10–15 minutes, stirring occasionally. Season to taste.

MICROWAVE: combine the oil, onion and garlic in a casserole and cook on HIGH power for 3 minutes. Stir in the herbs, carrot and mushrooms, cover and cook on HIGH power for 4 minutes, then stir in the minced beef, cover and cook on HIGH power for 5 minutes, stirring halfway through cooking. Finally stir in the remaining ingredients, cover and cook on HIGH power for 10–12 minutes, stirring occasionally.

LAMB FRIED WITH ONIONS

**Serves 2 / Preparation: 10 minutes plus standing /
Cooking: 10 minutes**

This is a dish inspired by the Mediterranean, where lamb is very popular. Serve it with a glass or two of wine as you settle down to watch your favourite travel programme. A Greek salad would complete the meal.

*1 × 350 g (12 oz) lamb fillet
1 clove garlic, crushed
30 ml (2 tbsp) lemon juice
5 ml (1 tsp) dried oregano
30–45 ml (2–3 tbsp) olive oil
1 large onion, sliced
salt and freshly ground black pepper*

1. Trim the fillet to remove fat and membrane. With a sharp knife, cut thinly into rounds. Place these in a single layer in a shallow dish. Add the garlic, sprinkle with the lemon juice and oregano and marinate for at least 20 minutes.
2. Heat 30 ml (2 tbsp) oil in a large frying pan and fry the onion rings until they begin to soften. Transfer the onion to a plate and set aside.
3. Add a little extra oil to that remaining in the pan if necessary, and place over moderate heat. Drain the meat and add it to the pan, turning it so that it browns quickly; this will take about 5 minutes. Return the onions to the pan and cook for 2 minutes more.
4. Season to taste and serve at once with Savoury rice (see page 85) or pitta bread to soak up the juices.

 # HOME-MADE BEEFBURGERS

Serves 4 / Preparation: 15 minutes / Cooking: 10–20 minutes

Home-made beefburgers are so much nicer than bought burgers and so easy to make. Make double the quantity and open freeze extras on freezer film before wrapping individually for storage. They may be cooked from frozen.

450 g (1 lb) minced beef
50 g (2 oz) fresh white or wholemeal breadcrumbs
1 onion, grated
2.5 ml (½ tsp) salt
freshly ground black pepper
1 egg

1. Combine all the ingredients in a large bowl and mix well, first with a fork and then with clean hands. Alternatively, use a mixer.
2. Divide the mixture into 4–8 pieces, rolling each to a ball. Flatten to beefburger shapes, using a burger press if you have one.
3. Grill for 4–5 minutes on each side or cook in a frying pan with a little oil. Alternatively, cook on a greased baking sheet in a preheated oven at 200°C (400°F), Gas Mark 6 for 15–20 minutes, depending on the size.

MICROWAVE: cook on HIGH power. Two beefburgers will require about 4 minutes, depending on size.

MEATBALLS WITH CHILLI SAUCE

Serves 4 / Preparation: 20 minutes / Cooking: 30 minutes

Meatballs cooked on a bed of onions and served with a chunky vegetable sauce will please the most critical consumers. For younger viewers – and tasters – vary the flavour by using half sausagemeat and half minced beef and omit the chilli from the sauce.

15 ml (1 tbsp) oil
1 onion, sliced
450 g (1 lb) minced beef
50 g (2 oz) fresh white or wholemeal breadcrumbs
15 ml (1 tbsp) chopped parsley
5 ml (1 tsp) dried oregano
salt and freshly ground black pepper
1 egg, lightly beaten

SAUCE
1 × 400 g (14 oz) can tomatoes
1 small onion, finely chopped
1 small green pepper, cored, seeded and chopped
5 ml (1 tsp) sugar
5 ml (1 tsp) chilli powder
45 ml (3 tbsp) red wine (optional)

1. Heat the oil in a saucepan, add the onion and cook gently until slightly softened. Arrange over the base of a shallow ovenproof dish.
2. In a bowl, combine the beef, breadcrumbs, parsley, oregano and seasoning. Mix well and bind with the egg.
3. Divide the mixture into eight portions and form into meatballs. Arrange in a single layer over the onion. Cook in a preheated oven at 200°C (400°F), Gas Mark 6 for 30 minutes, turning halfway through cooking.
4. Meanwhile, combine all the sauce ingredients in a saucepan. Bring to the boil, then lower the heat and simmer gently for 20–25 minutes. Pour into a sauceboat and serve with the meatballs.

MICROWAVE: cook the sliced onion in the oil in a shallow dish on HIGH power for 3 minutes. Make the meatballs as in steps 2 and 3, add them to the dish, then cook on HIGH power for 6 minutes, turning halfway through cooking. Cover and leave to stand while mixing all the sauce ingredients in a large jug and cooking on HIGH power for 5 minutes. Stir the sauce halfway through cooking. Pour the sauce over the meatballs, then cook the whole dish on HIGH power for 5 minutes more.

BEEF IN BEER

Serves 4 / Preparation: 15 minutes / Cooking: 2½ hours

After a long walk in the country, there's nothing nicer than relaxing in front of the TV with a hearty stew cooked in your absence. Dumplings would complete the meal, but if you don't feel up to making them, put some jacket potatoes in the oven at the same time as the stew.

50 g (2 oz) lard or dripping
1 large onion, chopped
2 carrots, scraped and sliced
2 sticks celery, sliced
15 ml (1 tbsp) plain flour.
salt and freshly ground black pepper
900 g (2 lb) braising steak, trimmed and cubed
450 ml (¾ pt) beer
15 ml (1 tbsp) tomato purée

1. Melt the lard in a large frying pan and quickly sauté the vegetables. Remove with a slotted spoon and place in a large casserole.
2. Place the flour in a plastic bag with seasoning, add the steak and toss until well coated. Brown the floured meat quickly in the fat remaining in the frying pan, then transfer with a slotted spoon to the casserole.
3. Pour over the beer and stir in the tomato purée. Cover and cook in a preheated oven at 150°C (300°F), Gas Mark 2 for 2–2½ hours or until the meat is tender. Season to taste and serve.

BOEUF STROGANOFF

Serves 2–3 / Preparation: 15 minutes / Cooking: 10 minutes

Although this is usually served as a dinner party dish, it is so easy to prepare that it is the ideal choice for a TV supper. Serve it with rice or buttered noodles.

450 g (1 lb) rump steak
40 g (1½ oz) butter
1 small onion, finely chopped
125 g (4 oz) button mushrooms, wiped and sliced
150 ml (5 fl oz) double cream
5 ml (1 tsp) Dijon mustard
salt and freshly ground black pepper

1. Place the steak between 2 sheets of dampened greaseproof paper and beat with a steak mallet or rolling pin until thin. Cut into narrow strips.
2. Melt the butter in a large frying pan, stir in the meat and cook quickly over high heat until browned all over. Remove the steak strips from the pan with a slotted spoon and keep warm.
3. Add the onion to the fat remaining in the pan and fry gently until soft. Stir in the mushrooms and cook for 2 minutes more, then stir in the cream and mustard and bring to the boil. Boil until slightly thickened.
4. Return the steak strips to the pan and stir gently. Season to taste and serve immediately.

MICROWAVE: follow step 1, then melt 25 g (1 oz) butter only in a casserole on HIGH power for 1 minute. Stir in the steak strips and cook on MEDIUM power for 5 minutes, stirring halfway through cooking. Remove the meat with a slotted spoon and keep warm. Add the onion to the casserole and cook on HIGH power for 2 minutes. Stir in the mushrooms and cook on HIGH power for a further 2 minutes. Add the cream and cook on HIGH power for 3 minutes, then stir in the steak strips and cook on HIGH power for 1 minute more. Lastly stir in the mustard, season to taste and serve.

SPANISH CHICKEN

Serves 4 / Preparation: 10 minutes / Cooking: 1–1½ hours

This is a very versatile recipe which can be cooked on the hob or in the oven and will not spoil if the TV programme you are watching goes on for longer than expected. Serve with rice or buttered noodles to mop up all the delicious juices.

15 ml (1 tbsp) oil
1 onion, sliced
1 clove garlic, crushed
1 red pepper, cored, seeded and sliced
1 green pepper, cored, seeded and sliced
125 g (4 oz) button mushrooms, wiped and sliced
1 × 400 g (14 oz) can tomatoes
150 ml (¼ pt) white wine or stock
2.5 ml (½ tsp) dried thyme
15 ml (1 tbsp) tomato purée
salt and freshly ground black pepper
4 chicken portions, skinned

1. Heat the oil in a large saucepan or flameproof casserole and gently fry the onion, garlic and peppers until soft. Add the mushrooms and cook for 2 minutes.
2. Stir in the tomatoes (with their juices), the wine, thyme, tomato purée and seasoning. Lastly add the chicken, turning over the joints in the sauce.
3. Cover, then simmer gently over low heat for 1–1½ hours or until the chicken is tender, turning the joints occasionally. Alternatively, cover and cook in a casserole in a preheated oven at 150°C (300°F), Gas Mark 2 for 1–1½ hours.

MICROWAVE: place the oil in a large casserole and stir in the onion, garlic and peppers. Cover and cook on HIGH power for 3 minutes. Stir in all the remaining ingredients, turning over the chicken in the sauce. Cover and cook on HIGH power for 30–35 minutes or until the chicken is tender and the juices run clear when the thickest part of the meat is tested with the tip of a sharp knife. Turn the joints occasionally.

CHICKEN CHOW MEIN

Serves 4 / Preparation: 10 minutes / Cooking: 10 minutes

Why bother with a take-away when this delicious Chinese dish can be put together in minutes? The instant egg noodles are an ideal ingredient to keep in the store cupboard and can form the basis of dozens of recipes. We used frozen bean sprouts as these are cheaper and more convenient than canned you can just use a handful and then replace the bag in the freezer. Do use fresh bean sprouts if available, as they have a crunchier texture.

125 g (4 oz) instant egg noodles
30 ml (2 tbsp) oil
1 clove garlic, crushed
1 onion, finely chopped
175 g (6 oz) button mushrooms, wiped and sliced
5 ml (1 tsp) cornflour
15 ml (1 tbsp) water
30 ml (2 tbsp) soy sauce
30 ml (2 tbsp) dry sherry
150 ml (¼ pt) chicken stock
175 g (6 oz) frozen or drained canned bean sprouts, or
125 g (4 oz) fresh bean sprouts
225 g (8 oz) cooked chicken, roughly chopped

1. Put the noodles in a saucepan or large bowl. Add plenty of boiling water to cover, then leave to stand for 4 minutes. Stir with a fork, then drain.
2. Heat the oil in a large frying pan or wok and gently fry the garlic and onion until soft. Stir in the mushrooms and cook for 2 minutes.
3. Meanwhile mix the cornflour to a paste with the water in a cup. Add the soy sauce, sherry and stock to the onion mixture and bring to the boil. Stir in the cornflour paste and allow the mixture to return to the boil, stirring constantly.
4. Stir in the noodles, bean sprouts and chicken and heat through thoroughly. Serve immediately.

MICROWAVE: prepare the noodles as in step 1. Combine the oil, garlic and onion in a large bowl and cook on HIGH power for 3 minutes. Stir in the mushrooms and cook on HIGH power for 2 minutes. In a cup, blend the cornflour with the soy sauce and add to the bowl with the sherry and stock. Cook on HIGH power for 4 minutes or until boiling, stirring halfway through cooking. Add the noodles, bean sprouts and chicken and cook for 4 minutes more on HIGH power, stirring occasionally.

PARMESAN-COATED CHICKEN DRUMSTICKS

Serves 4 / Preparation: 10 minutes / Cooking: 40 minutes

Adults and children alike will enjoy the contrast of crisp cheese coating and tender chicken in these tasty pick-up chicks. Just make sure you have plenty of paper napkins as holders and wipes. If possible, buy the Parmesan in the piece. Well-wrapped, it will keep in the refrigerator for a couple of weeks, and the flavour will be much better when you grate it yourself.

25 g (1 oz) fine soft white breadcrumbs
50 g (2 oz) Parmesan cheese, grated
1 clove garlic, crushed (optional)
2.5 ml (½ tsp) mixed dried herbs
salt and freshly ground black pepper
8 chicken drumsticks, skinned
25 g (1 oz) butter
15 ml (1 tbsp) oil

1. Combine the breadcrumbs, cheese, garlic (if used), herbs and seasoning in a shallow dish.
2. Roll the drumsticks in the crumb mixture until they are well coated, then set aside on a sheet of greaseproof paper.
3. Melt the butter with the oil in a roasting tin over moderate heat. Add the drumsticks and roast in a preheated hot oven 200°C (400°F), Gas Mark 6 for 40 minutes, turning halfway through cooking. Serve at once.

MICROWAVE: skin the drumsticks and arrange like the spokes of a wheel on a large plate, with the bone towards the centre. Cook on HIGH power for 12–15 minutes depending on size, turning the chicken once or twice. They will be rather pale in colour; 2.5 ml (½ tsp) paprika added to the coating mixture will improve their appearance.

TIP: to keep mess to a minimum, mix all the coating ingredients in a plastic bag, drop the chicken drumsticks in and shake.

CHICKEN AND BACON GOUGERE

Serves 4 / Preparation: 20 minutes / Cooking: 25 minutes

Many people shy away from making choux pastry but it can be prepared in less time than it takes to peel potatoes!

CHOUX PASTRY
65 g (2½ oz) plain flour
150 ml (¼ pt) water
50 g (2 oz) butter
2 eggs (size 3), lightly beaten
50 g (2 oz) Cheddar cheese, grated

FILLING
25 g (1 oz) butter
1 small onion, finely chopped
175 g (6 oz) smoked back bacon, rind removed and chopped
125 g (4 oz) button mushrooms, wiped and sliced
225 g (8 oz) cooked chicken, roughly chopped
15 ml (1 tbsp) plain flour
300 ml (½ pt) chicken stock
10 ml (2 tsp) tomato purée
salt and freshly ground black pepper
butter for greasing

1. Make the pastry. Place the flour on a sheet of greaseproof paper. Combine the water and butter in a small saucepan and bring to the boil. Boil until the butter has melted, then remove from the heat and immediately shoot in all the flour.
2. Beat until the mixture leaves the sides of the pan, if necessary returning to the heat for 1 minute. Allow to cool for 1 minute, then beat in the eggs a little at a time, beating thoroughly after each addition. Beat in the cheese, then set aside.
3. Make the filling. Melt the butter in a saucepan. Gently fry the onion and bacon until the onion is soft. Stir in the mushrooms and cook for 2 minutes.
4. Stir in the chicken and flour. Cook for 1 minute, then gradually stir in the stock. Bring to the boil, stirring constantly. Stir in the tomato purée and season to taste.
5. Divide the filling between 4 buttered, shallow individual dishes. Pipe or spoon the choux pastry around the edge of each dish in a continuous strip, to form a border, then bake in a preheated oven at 220°C (425°F), Gas Mark 7 for 20–25 minutes or until the pastry is well risen and golden brown.

MICROWAVE: the choux pastry may be made in the microwave by boiling the water and butter on HIGH power for 3–4 minutes, then following the instructions in steps 1 and 2. To make the filling, melt the butter in a bowl on HIGH power for 1 minute. Stir in the onion and bacon and cook on HIGH power for 3 minutes. Stir in the mushrooms and cook on HIGH power for 2 minutes. Add the chicken, blend in the flour then stir in the stock. Cook on HIGH power for 4–5 minutes, stirring halfway through cooking. Finally stir in the tomato purée and seasoning. Bake the completed dish in a conventional oven.

TIP: another delicious recipe for choux pastry. Cook small buns by dropping the mixture by teaspoons on to a baking sheet and cooking in a preheated oven at 180°C (350°F), Gas Mark 4 for 15–30 minutes. Slit the buns to allow steam to escape, then cool and freeze. These may then be crisped from frozen in a hot oven. Fill with a savoury mixture or with whipped cream for a tempting dessert topped with chocolate sauce.

PAN-FRIED TURKEY WITH SAGE

Serves 2 / Preparation: 10 minutes / Cooking: 6 minutes

Turkey breast is now available in most supermarkets; if you can't get it, chicken is equally suitable. Cooking it this way seals in the flavour and takes very little time, making it ideal for those occasions when you want something substantial in a hurry. Serve it with buttered noodles and a green salad.

2 × 125 g (4 oz) turkey fillets
15 ml (1 tbsp) plain flour
salt and freshly ground black pepper
2.5 ml (½ tsp) dried sage
25 g (1 oz) butter
15 ml (1 tbsp) oil
fresh sage leaves to garnish

1. Put the turkey between 2 sheets of greaseproof paper or cling film and gently bat out with a rolling pin until it is flat and thin.
2. Mix the flour, seasoning and sage in a plastic bag. Add the pieces of turkey and shake gently until evenly coated.
3. Melt the butter in the oil in a frying pan. When the fat is hot, add the escolopes, browning them quickly on both sides, then lower the heat and cook for 1–2 minutes more until cooked through.
4. Serve immediately, garnished with the fresh sage leaves.

VEGETABLE CURRY

Serves 4 / Preparation: 15 minutes / Cooking: 15 minutes

A change in the weather can create problems for the most organised cook. That superb salad may not seem as appropriate when it is pouring with rain. Substitute something hot and spicy, such as this excellent vegetarian curry, and your guests will view you with admiration. Curry paste gives a particularly good flavour but if you prefer to make your own curry powder combine 5 ml (1 tsp) each of turmeric, ground coriander and cumin with 2.5 ml (½ tsp) ground fenugreek and 1.25 ml (¼ tsp) chilli powder.

40 g (1½ oz) butter
1 onion, chopped
40 g (1½ oz) plain flour
15 ml (1 tbsp) curry paste
15 ml (1 tbsp) tomato purée
600 ml (1 pt) hot vegetable stock
1 small cauliflower, cut into small florets
450 g (1 lb) courgettes, sliced
1 × 425 g (15 oz) can chick peas, drained

1. Melt the butter in a large saucepan and gently fry the onion until soft. Stir in the flour and cook for 1 minute.
2. Gradually stir in the curry paste, tomato purée and stock, then bring to the boil, stirring constantly.
3. Stir in the cauliflower and courgettes, bring to the boil then lower the heat, cover and simmer for 10 minutes or until the cauliflower is tender. Stir in the chick peas, heat through and serve.

MICROWAVE: place the cauliflower in a bowl with 45 ml (3 tbsp) water. Cover and cook on HIGH power for 3 minutes, then drain and set aside. Melt the butter in a large casserole on HIGH power for 1 minute, then stir in the onion and cook on HIGH power for 3 minutes. Stir in the flour. Gradually stir in the curry paste, tomato purée and stock. Cook on HIGH power for 4 minutes, whisking thoroughly halfway through cooking and again on completion. Stir in the courgettes and cauliflower, cover and cook on HIGH power for 8 minutes or until the vegetables are just tender. Stir in the chick peas and cook on HIGH power for 2 minutes more.

BAKED KIBBEH

**Serves 6 / Preparation: 20 minutes plus soaking /
Cooking: 50 minutes**

This dish owes its origins to Syrian traditional cooking. It would normally be made into fat cigar shapes and deep fried. Our way is less fiddly and lower in calories. Serve with a salad and a pot of Greek strained yogurt.

175g (6 oz) bulgur (cracked wheat)
2 large onions, finely chopped
450 g (1 lb) minced lamb
5 ml (1 tsp) salt
freshly ground black pepper
15 ml (1 tbsp) olive oil
10 ml (2 tsp) curry powder
10 ml (2 tsp) tomato purée
50 g (2 oz) pine kernels or chopped walnuts
300 ml (½ pt) beef stock
25 g (1 oz) butter
oil for greasing

1. Cover the cracked wheat with cold water and soak for 30 minutes, then drain, squeezing out as much water as possible. Transfer to a bowl and add half the onion, half the lamb and 2.5 ml (½ tsp) salt. Mix well, adding a grinding of black pepper.
2. Heat the oil in a large frying pan and fry the remaining lamb and onion for 5 minutes. Stir the remaining salt, the curry powder, the tomato purée and half the pine kernels into the hot mixture, with freshly ground black pepper to taste.
3. Place half the cracked wheat mixture in a greased 20 cm(8 in) square dish, cover with the fried mixture and top with the remaining cracked wheat mixture. Level the surface.
4. Score diagonal lines across the top of the mixture and sprinkle on the remaining pine kernels. Pour over half the stock and dot with all the butter. Bake in a preheated oven at 200°C (400°F), Gas Mark 6 for 50 minutes, basting halfway through with the remaining stock.

MICROWAVE: follow step 1, then mix the oil with the remaining lamb and onion in a bowl and cook in the microwave for 5 minutes on HIGH power. Proceed as in the recipe, cooking the assembled dish in a conventional oven.

LAYERED PARSNIP AND CHEESE BAKE

Serves 4 / Preparation: 15 minutes / Cooking: 40 minutes

The sweetness of the parsnips gives this casserole an unusual flavour. It may be served as a vegetable accompaniment, but we think it is good enough for a starring role.

45 ml (3 tbsp) oil
900 g (2 lb) parsnips, peeled and thinly sliced
1 × 400 g (14 oz) can tomatoes, drained and roughly chopped
salt and freshly ground black pepper
175 g (6 oz) Cheddar cheese, grated
300 ml (10 fl oz) single cream
50 g (2 oz) fresh white breadcrumbs
25 g (1 oz) butter
butter for greasing

1. Heat the oil in a large saucepan and gently fry the parsnips for 5 minutes.
2. Arrange one third of the parsnips over the base of a greased 1.75 litre (3 pt) casserole.
3. Cover with one third of the tomatoes. Season to taste, then sprinkle over one third of the cheese and one third of the cream. Repeat the layers until the ingredients are used up.
4. Sprinkle over the breadcrumbs, dot with butter and bake in a preheated oven at 160°C (325°F), Gas Mark 3 for 40 minutes or until the parsnips are tender.

COWBOY BEANS

**Serves 4 / Preparation: 10 minutes plus overnight soaking /
Cooking: 1½ hours**

In every Western you ever watch, cowboys eat beans. Apart from them being easy to store it is difficult to see why: their long soaking and cooking times must have been a nightmare over a camp fire! Fortunately we have more modern means of cooking, so can enjoy this hearty dish whenever we can muster the ingredients.

225 g (8 oz) dried pinto, haricot, borlotti or black-eyed beans
30 ml (2 tbsp) oil
1 large onion, chopped
1 × 400 g (14 oz) can tomatoes
225 g (8 oz) bacon in a piece
2.5 ml (½ tsp) mixed dried herbs
5 ml (1 tsp) sugar
10 ml (2 tsp) tomato purée
salt and freshly ground black pepper

1. Place the beans in a bowl with cold water to cover. Leave to soak overnight, changing the water several times.
2. Drain the beans and place in a large saucepan. Cover with plenty of fresh water. Bring to the boil, boil hard for 5 minutes, then lower the heat and simmer for 40 minutes or until the beans are tender but not mushy. The time will depend on the type and age of the beans. When cooked, drain the beans, reserving 600 ml (1 pt) of the cooking water.
3. Heat the oil in a large saucepan and fry the onion until soft. Add the beans, tomatoes (with their juice), the bacon, reserved bean water, herbs, sugar and tomato purée. Do not add seasoning at this stage as it would toughen the beans.
4. Bring the mixture to the boil, lower the heat and simmer gently for 40 minutes, adding more liquid if necessary.
5. Season to taste. If the mixture is too runny boil furiously to evaporate.
6. Remove the bacon with a slotted spoon and slice to serve with the beans.

PEANUT PAELLA

Serves 4 / Preparation: 15 minutes / Cooking: 20–25 minutes

You won't find this paella on the menu in Malaga, but it's very good for all that. It is much cheaper to make than the traditional dish and although it was created with vegetarians in view, it is sufficiently tasty for non-vegetarians to enjoy without feeling deprived.

450 g (1 lb) brown rice
15 ml (1 tbsp) sunflower oil
1 onion, finely chopped
5 sticks celery, sliced
1 red pepper, cored, seeded and sliced
1 × 400 g (14 oz) can tomatoes
500 ml (18 fl oz) vegetable stock
175 g (6 oz) salted peanuts
salt and freshly ground black pepper
15 ml (1 tbsp) chopped parsley
10 ml (2 tsp) grated lemon rind

1. Soak the rice in a bowl with cold water to cover for 15 minutes.
2. Meanwhile heat the oil in a saucepan and sauté the onion for 5 minutes over low heat. Add the celery and red pepper and cook for a further 4 minutes.
3. With a sharp knife, chop up the tomatoes in the can. Add with their juices to the pan with the stock. Drain the rice and stir it in to the pan. Bring to the boil, lower the heat, cover and simmer very gently for 25–30 minutes, stirring several times, until the rice is just tender.
4. Remove the rice from the heat and leave to stand for 5 minutes, by which time all liquid should be absorbed and the rice should be fluffy. If not, cook it a little longer.
5. Stir in the peanuts and season to taste.
6. Just before serving, combine the parsley and lemon rind in a small bowl. Mix well and sprinkle over the rice.

> MICROWAVE: follow step 1, then place the oil and onion in a large bowl and cook on HIGH power for 3 mintues; add the celery and pepper and cook for a further 3 minutes. Add the tomatoes, stock and drained rice as in step 3 but do not cover the bowl. Cook on HIGH power for 25 minutes, stirring once. Cover and proceed as in steps 4–6.

✓ *LENTIL AND BULGUR LOAF*

Serves 6 / Preparation: 35 minutes
Cooking: 45–50 minutes

Bulgur gives this loaf a crunchy texture that contrasts well with the creamy lentils. It may be served hot or cold.

50 g (2 oz) bulgur or cracked wheat
175 g (6 oz) red lentils
350 ml (12 fl oz) water
1 onion, finely chopped
175 g (6 oz) tomatoes, skinned (see page 33) and chopped
125 g (4 oz) Cheddar cheese, grated
2.5 ml (½ tsp) cayenne pepper
salt
1 egg, lightly beaten
oil for greasing

1. Place the bulgur in a bowl with cold water to cover. Leave to soak for 30 minutes.
2. Rinse the lentils under cold water, drain, then place in a large saucepan. Add the measured water, cover and simmer for 10–15 minutes or until the mixture resembles a thick purée. Remove from the heat.
3. Drain the bulgur and add to the lentils with the remaining ingredients. Mix thoroughly.
4. Spoon the mixture into a greased 900 g (2 lb) loaf tin and bake in a preheated oven at 190°C (375°F), Gas Mark 5 for 45–50 minutes. Leave to stand for 10 minutes before turning out on a platter to serve.

MICROWAVE: follow step 1, then rinse the lentils and place in a large casserole with the measured water. Cook uncovered on HIGH power for 8–10 minutes, adding a little more water if necessary, until a thick purée is formed. Follow step 3. Spoon into a greased 900 g (2 lb) loaf dish, cover and cook on MEDIUM power for 12–15 minutes or until set.

Add herbs, mushrooms to liven it up

SUPPORTING FEATURES

*E*very good meal needs its supporting feature; accompaniments and accessories without whose contribution the occasion would be less of a success. In this section you'll find new ways with potatoes, splendid salads and versatile vegetable dishes, plus dressings and sauces to add zest and the element of the unexpected. One of the problems with TV dinners is that they have to compete for your attention. Add these recipes to your repertoire of main attractions and what is off screen will be just as exciting as what's on!

CASSEROLED POTATOES

Serves 4 / Preparation: 5 minutes / Cooking: 50 minutes

This is one of our favourite ways of cooking potatoes, mainly because it is so easy. It requires no attention once it has started to cook and will not spoil if the TV programme you are watching is too gripping to leave! While this is best with new potatoes, it works well with small old potatoes. For a delicious variation, add as many peeled whole cloves of garlic as you dare.

675 g (1½ lb) new potatoes
25 g (1 oz) butter
30 ml (2 tbsp) water
salt and freshly ground black pepper
2.5 ml (½ tsp) dried mixed herbs or a bunch of fresh herbs

1. Scrub the potatoes well but do not peel.
2. Place them in a casserole with all the other ingredients and cover closely with greaseproof paper or foil and a lid.
3. Bake in a preheated oven at 180°C (350°F), Gas Mark 4 for about 50 minutes or until the potatoes are tender. Timing will depend upon the size of the potatoes. Serve from the casserole, with the juices.

RÖSTI CAKES

Serves 4 / Preparation: 10 minutes / Cooking: 10 minutes

This is an interesting way of serving potatoes. Flour is used to bind the mixture but with floury potatoes, this may not be necessary. Cheese is an optional addition. The mixture cooks to crisp strands of potato that look most attractive.

675 g (1½ lb) old potatoes
1 onion, grated
2.5 ml (½ tsp) salt
freshly ground black pepper to taste
125 g (4 oz) Jarlsberg or Edam cheese, grated
15 ml (1 tbsp) plain flour
1 egg, beaten

1. Peel the potatoes and grate them into a sieve. Rinse in cold water and drain thoroughly, pressing the mixture against the sides of the sieve. Tip into a bowl.
2. Mix in the onion, seasoning, cheese, flour and egg and mix well.
3. Pour enough oil into a large frying pan to cover the base. Heat the oil, then add the potato mixture in large spoonfuls to make individual cakes. Flatten the cakes slightly with a palette knife and cook until they are brown on both sides. Repeat with the rest of the mixture. Alternatively spoon the mixture as before on to a well greased baking sheet and bake in a preheated oven at 220°C (425°F), Gas Mark 7 for 20–25 minutes. Serve.

SPICED POTATO STICKS

Serves 4 / Preparation: 10 minutes / Cooking: 20–30 minutes

Our version of oven chips with a kick! They will really liven up an otherwise plain meal or may be eaten as a nibble with cocktails.

675 g (1½ lb) potatoes
30 ml (2 tbsp) oil
5 ml (1 tsp) ground cumin
2.5 ml (½ tsp) ground coriander
2.5 ml (½ tsp) cayenne
salt

1. Peel the potatoes, slice 5 mm (¼ in) thick, then cut into matchsticks.
2. Place all the remaining ingredients in a mixing bowl and stir in the potato sticks. Toss until the sticks are well coated.
3. Spread the potato sticks in a single layer on the base of a large roasting tin. Cook in a preheated oven at 220°C (425°F), Gas Mark 7 for 20–30 minutes, or until crisp and golden brown. Turn occasionally.

STIR-FRY

Serves 4 / Preparation: 20 minutes / Cooking: 10–15 minutes

The cardinal rule with a stir-fry is to cut the vegetables up finely so that they cook quickly, while remaining slightly crisp.

30 ml (2 tbsp) olive oil
1 clove garlic, crushed
10 ml (2 tsp) finely grated fresh root ginger (optional)
1 onion, finely chopped
225 g (8 oz) carrots, scraped and cut into matchsticks
1 small cauliflower, broken into small florets
225 g (8 oz) courgettes, sliced
125 g (4 oz) button mushrooms, wiped and sliced
15–30 ml (1–2 tbsp) soy sauce

1. Heat the oil in a large frying pan or wok and quickly fry the garlic and ginger. Stir in the onion, carrots and cauliflower and cook over a moderate heat for 5 minutes, constantly turning over with a wooden spatula.
2. Stir in the courgettes and mushrooms and continue to cook, stirring all the time, until the vegetables are just beginning to soften.
3. Stir in the soy sauce, heat through and serve with Savoury rice.

SAVOURY RICE

Serves 4 / Preparation: 5 minutes / Cooking: 20 minutes

A good savoury rice is the ideal accompaniment, especially if the main dish is spicy or has lots of sauce. You will find the flavour of the rice much improved by 'toasting' in the oil. This also helps to keep the grains separate, so the result is a light, fluffy rice.

15 ml (1 tbsp) oil
1 onion, finely chopped
1½ cups (285 g/10½ oz) long-grain rice
3 cups (750 ml/1¼ pt) boiling water or stock
salt
225 g (8 oz) frozen mixed vegetables

1. Heat the oil in a saucepan and stir in the onion and rice. Cook over a fairly high heat, stirring constantly until the rice is lightly toasted.
2. Remove the pan from the heat and carefully add the boiling water or stock. The fat will splatter a little at first, so take care! Season with salt.
3. Bring the rice to the boil, then lower the heat, cover and simmer gently until almost all the water has been absorbed. Stir in the vegetables and continue to cook gently until all the water has been absorbed and the vegetables are tender.

MICROWAVE: the rice may be cooked in the microwave although it is not possible to reproduce the toasting effect. The grains, however, will be light and separate. Place the oil and onion in a casserole and cook on HIGH power for 3 minutes. Stir in the rice, water or stock and seasoning. Cover and cook on HIGH power for 12 minutes. Stir in the vegetables, then cover and leave to stand for 5 minutes. If the vegetables are not cooked, return to the microwave on HIGH power for a further 2–3 minutes.

BUTTERED PASTA

Serves 2 / Cooking: 12 minutes

Pasta's popularity is not surprising. It is swift and simple to cook, a pleasure to eat and enormously varied. In Britain alone there are more than thirty different shapes and sizes. When cooking pasta, allow 50–75 g (2–3 oz) per person and cook it in plenty of boiling salted water. A spoonful of oil will help to prevent the pasta from sticking together. The method of cooking outlined below works extremely well with most types and the pasta needs no watching. Do use fresh pasta, if available, but reduce the cooking time. It should be cooked in boiling water and is ready when it rises to the surface. This may only take a few minutes, so check it frequently.

1.5 litres (2½ pt) water
15 ml (1 tbsp) oil
salt
175 g (6 oz) pasta
25 g (1 oz) butter
freshly ground black pepper

1. Bring the water to the boil in a large saucepan. Stir in the oil, with 5 ml (1 tsp) salt. Add the pasta. Stir.
2. Bring the pasta back to the boil, cover the saucepan and remove from the heat.
3. Leave for 12 minutes, then drain the pasta in a colander. Tip into a bowl, add the butter and season to taste.

> MICROWAVE: this may be cooked in a bowl in the microwave but there is no advantage in terms of time.

RATATOUILLE

**Serves 4 / Preparation: 5 minutes plus standing /
Cooking: 35 minutes**

This recipe originated in Provence in the south of France. It is basically a casserole of vegetables which may be served hot or cold and as it is so well flavoured it complements grilled meats, chicken or fish. It also makes a tasty filling for vols-au-vent or crêpes. Fresh tomatoes are traditionally used, but for the sake of convenience we have used canned.

*1 large aubergine
salt and freshly ground black pepper
45 ml (3 tbsp) oil, preferably olive oil
1 large onion, sliced
2 cloves garlic, crushed
1 red pepper, cored, seeded and sliced
1 green pepper, cored, seeded and sliced
225 g (8 oz) courgettes, sliced
1 × 400 g (14 oz) can tomatoes, drained*

1. Slice the aubergine into a colander, sprinkle with salt and leave to stand for 30 minutes. Rinse thoroughly with cold water, then pat dry with absorbent kitchen paper.
2. Heat the oil in a large saucepan and fry the onion and garlic for 2–3 minutes. Stir in the aubergine with the remaining ingredients, then cover and simmer gently for 30–35 minutes.

MICROWAVE: follow step 1, then place the oil in a large casserole, stir in the onion and garlic and cook on HIGH power for 3 minutes. Stir in the aubergine with the remaining ingredients, cover and cook on HIGH power for 20–25 minutes, stirring halfway through cooking.

TIP: to make a delicious Courgettes Provençale, replace the aubergine and peppers with an extra 225 g (8 oz) of courgettes and simmer for 10–15 minutes.

GOLDEN VEGETABLES

Serves 4 / Preparation: 10 minutes / Cooking: 20 minutes

Go for gold with this nutritious dish that is enjoyed even by children who say they hate carrots or swedes. It appeals to more sophisticated palates, too. Don't be tempted to substitute margarine for the butter (the flavour will suffer) and be sure to add plenty of freshly ground black pepper. Serve it as a substitute for creamed potatoes; it is particularly good with sausages and fried eggs.

225 g (8 oz) swede, peeled and diced
225 g (8 oz) carrots, scraped and sliced
225 g (8 oz) potatoes, peeled and cubed
salt and freshly ground black pepper
50 g (2 oz) butter

1. Bring a saucepan of salted water to the boil and add the swede and carrots. Cook for 2–3 minutes, then add the potato cubes.
2. Lower the heat and simmer gently until all the vegetables are tender. Drain the vegetables and place them in a bowl, reserving the cooking water for a soup or gravy.
3. Mash the vegetables, season to taste and stir in the butter.

MICROWAVE: cut the vegetables into small pieces and place in a casserole with 60 ml (4 tbsp) water. Cook on HIGH power for 12–15 minutes or until tender, stirring once or twice during cooking. Drain and mash with the butter.

SHREDDED VEGETABLES

Serves 4 / Preparation: 10 minutes / Cooking: 5 minutes

This delicious vegetable dish can be prepared in seconds with the aid of a slicer shredder; if you do not have one, a coarse grater works equally well. In selecting your trio of vegetables, try to choose contrasting colours. Carrot, celery and runner beans make a good combination as do carrots, courgettes, and parsnips.

Pick THREE of the following vegetables;
225 g (8 oz) carrots, scraped and grated
225 g (8 oz) courgettes, grated
225 g (8 oz) parsnips, peeled and grated
225 g (8 oz) turnips, peeled and grated
225 g (8 oz) swede, peeled and grated
225 g (8 oz) runner beans, trimmed and finely sliced
225 g (8 oz) celery, finely sliced
25 g (1 oz) butter
60 ml (4 tbsp) water
salt and freshly ground black pepper

1. Place your three chosen vegetables in a saucepan with a well-fitting lid and add the butter and water.
2. Cover the pan and simmer gently, shaking once or twice for 5 minutes, or until the vegetables are tender. Season to taste and serve.

MICROWAVE: follow the instructions above but cook the vegetables in a casserole and use only 30 ml (2 tbsp) water. Cook on HIGH power for 5 minutes, stirring once.

CELERY AU GRATIN

Serves 4 / Preparation: 10 minutes / Cooking: 20 minutes

Celery is generally under-used as a hot vegetable, which is a shame as it can provide such an interesting accompaniment to a simple main course. Fresh celery does need braising if it is to be tender, but here we cheat and use canned celery hearts. As this is a rich vegetable dish it should be served with something simple such as grilled meat or fish.

2 × 425 g (15 oz) cans celery hearts, drained
150 ml (5 fl oz) double cream
salt and freshly ground black pepper
50 g (2 oz) Cheddar cheese, grated

1. Pat the celery hearts dry with absorbent kitchen paper, then arrange in a shallow ovenproof dish.
2. Pour the cream into a jug, season generously, then pour over the celery. Sprinkle with the grated cheese and bake in a preheated oven at 200°C (400°F), Gas Mark 6 for 15–20 minutes or until beginning to brown.

> MICROWAVE: follow steps 1 and 2, but cook on HIGH power for 6–8 minutes, or until the cream and cheese are bubbling.

ZAMBIAN CABBAGE

Serves 4 / Preparation: 5 minutes / Cooking: 5 minutes

This cabbage recipe was inspired by a vegetable relish eaten in Zambia. It would normally be very well cooked and eaten with *nshima*, a type of porridge made from maize. We prefer our cabbage with a bit of a bite, but whether crunchy or creamy, it tastes delicious with sausages and mash or chops. Because the cabbage is cooked in its own juices, it is particularly tasty and retains the maximum amount of vitamins and minerals.

30 ml (2 tbsp) oil
1 onion, finely chopped
450 g (1 lb) Savoy or spring cabbage, shredded
2 tomatoes, chopped
salt and freshly ground black pepper

1. Heat the oil in a large saucepan, add the onion and cook gently for a few minutes until beginning to soften.
2. Wash the shredded cabbage in plenty of cold water. Shake off most of the water, but do not dry.
3. Add the cabbage and tomatoes to the pan and stir well, then cover and cook over very low heat, stirring once or twice, for 5 minutes or until the cabbage is cooked.
4. Season to taste and serve immediately.

MICROWAVE: this cooks well in the microwave. Cook the onions and oil in a casserole on HIGH power for 4 minutes. Add the washed cabbage and tomatoes and cook for a further 5 minutes on HIGH power or until the cabbage is cooked.

THREE BEAN SALAD

Serves 4 / Preparation: 10 minutes

Proof that the store cupboard can yield a super salad is provided by this colourful accompaniment. Many different types of canned bean are now available and you may like to experiment with some of the more unusual varieties.

1 × 283 g (10 oz) can broad beans, drained and rinsed
1 × 283 g (10 oz) can cut green beans, drained and rinsed
1 × 213 g (8 oz) can butter beans, drained and rinsed

DRESSING
15 ml (1 tbsp) olive oil
7.5 ml (1½ tsp) wine vinegar
5 ml (1 tsp) Dijon mustard
2.5 ml (½ tsp) caster sugar
salt and freshly ground black pepper

1. Drain the rinsed beans thoroughly, then combine in a serving dish.
2. Whisk all the dressing ingredients together in a jug or shake in a screw-topped jar. Pour over the beans, toss lightly, then serve.

MARINATED MUSHROOM SALAD

Serves 4 with other salads / Preparation: 10 minutes

Serve a selection of summer salads as a movable feast on those evenings when you would rather be watching the television than standing in the kitchen. This mushroom salad would be an ideal choice. It may be made in advance and stored in the refrigerator for a couple of days. Mushrooms shrink once cooked or marinated, so this does not make a huge quantity. Double up on the mushrooms if you want generous portions.

225 g (8 oz) button mushrooms, wiped
120 ml/4 fl oz Vinaigrette (see page 94)
15 ml (1 tbsp) chopped parsley

1. If the mushrooms are large, cut them in halves or quarters. Small mushrooms may be left whole.
2. Place the mushrooms in a bowl with a lid. Pour on the vinaigrette and add the parsley. Stir well or shake to mix. Cover the bowl and marinate for at least 2 hours, stirring or shaking occasionally.

CUCUMBER AND YOGURT SALAD

Serves 2–4 / Preparation: 5 minutes plus chilling

Variations on this recipe are found all over the Mediterranean and India. It is called *tzatziki* in Greece and *raitha* in India. Ring the changes by adding a little garlic or chopped chilli, a few drops of olive oil or by changing the mint for dill – it remains a refreshing starter or accompaniment to curries, grilled lamb or kibbeh (page 77).

½ cucumber, grated
½ small onion, grated
15 ml (1 tbsp) chopped fresh mint
150 ml (5 fl oz) plain yogurt
salt and freshly ground black pepper to taste

1. Mix all the ingredients together in a small bowl, cover and chill for 30 minutes before serving.

VINAIGRETTE

Makes 250 ml (8 fl oz) / Preparation: 5 minutes

This may not be the classic French dressing or vinaigrette but it is delicious and works very well. The onion thickens the mixture and helps it go further, so less oil is needed. If possible, make it in a blender or food processor and keep it in a screw-top jar for up to a week, shaking it well before serving. The basic recipe may be varied by the addition of a chopped clove of garlic, a bunch of parsley or other herbs before blending. Experiment with different vinegars and oils to change the flavour or try replacing part of the vinegar with a little orange or lemon juice.

175 ml (6 fl oz) sunflower oil
75 ml (5 tbsp) wine vinegar
5 ml (1 tsp) mustard powder
5 ml (1 tsp) sugar
2.5 ml (½ tsp) salt
2.5 ml (½ tsp) freshly ground black pepper
1 small onion, roughly chopped

1. Combine all the ingredients in the bowl of a blender or food processor and blend until smooth. Alternatively, chop the onion very finely and mix all the ingredients by shaking vigorously in a screw-topped jar.
2. Pour into a screw top jar and use as required.

BLUE CHEESE DRESSING

Makes about 275 ml (9 fl oz) / Preparation: 5 minutes

Power dressing which will improve the image of the most boring salad! It is also excellent when spooned over a hamburger or steak. To transform it to a hot sauce to serve with steak, crumble the cheese into the cream and heat gently in a saucepan. Season with freshly ground black pepper, but leave out the lemon juice and olive oil.

75 g (3 oz) Stilton cheese
150 ml (5 fl oz) double cream
5 ml (1 tsp) lemon juice
5 ml (1 tsp) olive oil
freshly ground black pepper

1. Crumble the cheese into a wide-mouthed jug and beat in the remaining ingredients. Use at once or store in the refrigerator until required.

THOUSAND ISLAND DRESSING

Makes about 200 ml (7 fl oz) / Preparation: 10 minutes

An American speciality which is delicious with mixed salads, prawn salads or hamburgers.

150 ml (¼ pt) mayonnaise
1 hard–boiled egg, finely chopped
30 ml (2 tbsp) sweet pickle, finely chopped
15 ml (1 tbsp) finely chopped onion
15 ml (1 tbsp) tomato ketchup
salt and freshly ground black pepper

1. Beat all the ingredients together in a wide-mouthed jug. Use at once or store in the refrigerator until required.

BARBECUE SAUCE

**Makes 300 ml (½ pt) / Preparation: 10 minutes /
Cooking: 20 minutes**

This sauce begs to be made in bulk for storage in usable quantities in the freezer. It will give the simplest meals immediate appeal. Try it on chicken portions, pork chops or steaks, breast of lamb or spare ribs. Spoon onto jacket potatoes or simmer a drained can of haricot or butter beans in the sauce for 15 minutes for a substantial accompaniment to sausages or bacon.

15 ml (1 tbsp) oil
1 onion, finely chopped
1 × 200 g (7 oz) can tomatoes
15 ml (1 tbsp) vinegar
15 ml (1 tbsp) soft light brown sugar
30 ml (2 tbsp) Worcestershire sauce
45 ml (3 tbsp) soy sauce
5 ml (1 tsp) prepared mustard
150 ml (¼ pt) water
15 ml (1 tbsp) tomato purée
10 ml (2 tsp) cornflour

1. Heat the oil in a saucepan and fry the onion until beginning to soften. Add the tomatoes, with their juices, then stir in all the other ingredients except the cornflour. Bring to the boil, lower the heat and simmer for 15 minutes.
2. Meanwhile place the cornflour in a cup and mix to a paste with a little extra water. Stir the paste into the tomato mixture. Return to the boil, lower the heat and simmer for 3 minutes, stirring constantly.

MICROWAVE: as above but cook in a casserole, allowing 4 minutes on HIGH power for the oil and onions. Then add the tomatoes and all other ingredients except the cornflour and cook for 10 minutes on HIGH power. Finally add the cornflour mixture and cook for another 4 minutes on HIGH power.

CHASSEUR SAUCE

**Makes about 600 ml (1 pt) / Preparation: 10 minutes /
Cooking: 30 minutes**

This is another easy sauce which is worth making in advance and freezing. Serve it with gammon steaks, sausages or chops or use as a basis for vegetarian meals.

30 ml (2 tbsp) olive oil
1 onion, chopped
2 sticks celery, finely sliced
75 g (3 oz) green pepper, cored, seeded and diced
125 g (4 oz) mushrooms, wiped and sliced
15 g (1 tbsp) plain flour
1 × 400 g (14 oz) can chopped tomatoes
120 ml (4 fl oz) water
5 ml (1 tsp) tomato purée
1.25 ml (¼ tsp) mixed dried herbs
salt and freshly ground black pepper to taste
5 ml (1 tsp) chopped parsley

1. Heat the oil in a saucepan and fry the onion until soft.
2. Stir in the celery, green pepper and mushrooms and cook gently for 3–4 minutes.
3. Add the flour and stir well. Remove from the heat and stir in all the remaining ingredients except the parsley.
4. Bring the mixture to the boil, lower the heat and simmer for 30 minutes. Finally, stir in the parsley, check the seasoning and serve.

MICROWAVE: this can easily be made in a microwave. Use a large bowl and cook the onion in the oil on HIGH power for 4 minutes. Add the celery, green pepper and mushrooms and cook on HIGH power for 4 minutes. Follow step 3, then cook on HIGH power for 10 minutes followed by MEDIUM power for 10 minutes.

TIP: for a simple supper, brown 4 lamb or pork chops and place them in a casserole. Prepare the sauce to the end of step 3, pour over the chops and cook in a preheated oven at 180°C (350°F), Gas Mark 4 for 45 minutes.

QUICK TOMATO SAUCE

Serves 4–6 / Preparation: 10 minutes / Cooking: 20 minutes

This is such a versatile sauce; it may be used on spaghetti, over sausages or beefburgers, with vegetables or even diluted with a little cream to make a tasty soup. Making it couldn't be simpler for the TV cook. Simply whoosh it up in one commercial break and simmer slowly until the next. If you don't possess a blender or food processor, chop the onion very finely and simmer the sauce for a little longer. Serve it as it is or push it through a sieve for a smooth sauce. We find it helpful to make it in bulk and freeze the surplus.

1 small onion, chopped
1 clove garlic, crushed (optional)
1 × 400 g (14 oz) can tomatoes
5 ml (1 tsp) sugar
1.25 ml (¼ tsp) mixed dried herbs
5 ml (1 tsp) tomato purée
250 ml (8 fl oz) water
salt and freshly ground black pepper to taste

1. Put all the ingredients except the salt and pepper into the bowl of a blender or food processor, and blend until smooth.
2. Pour the tomato sauce into a saucepan and bring to the boil. Lower the heat and simmer uncovered for 15 minutes or until thickened; season to taste.

MICROWAVE: follow the directions above, but use a bowl and cook on HIGH power for 5 minutes, then for 10 minutes on MEDIUM power.

PEPPER SAUCE

**Makes about 500 ml (18 fl oz) / Preparation: 5 minutes /
Cooking: 5 minutes**

This useful sauce may be served with anything from a beefburger to a fillet
steak. For steak though, we would be tempted to replace half the stock with
red wine.

25 g (1 oz) butter
125 g (4 oz) green pepper, cored, seeded and chopped
50 g (2 oz) button mushrooms, wiped and sliced
15 ml (1 tbsp) plain flour
300 ml (½ pt) hot beef or vegetable stock
15 ml (1 tbsp) tomato purée
salt and freshly ground black pepper

1. Melt the butter in a saucepan and gently fry the pepper until soft. Stir in
the mushrooms and cook for 1 minute, then stir in the flour.
2. Gradually stir in the stock and tomato purée, then bring to the boil,
stirring constantly. Season to taste and serve in a sauceboat.

MICROWAVE: melt the butter in a large jug on HIGH power for 1 minute. Stir
in the pepper and cook on HIGH power for 3 minutes. Stir in the mushrooms
and cook on HIGH power for 1 minute. Stir in the flour, then gradually blend
in the stock and tomato purée. Cook on HIGH power for 3 minutes, stirring
halfway through cooking. Season to taste.

HAPPY ENDINGS

*E*veryone loves a happy ending and you'll find more than twenty-five here, from Strawberry and orange brûlée to Spicy peaches and irresistible Chocolate and chestnut pots.

Whether you are feasting alone, taking solace in strudel or sharing a Deb's delight, you'll soon be coming back for seconds. Biscuits, cakes, crumbles; they are all here, plus a few puddings specially selected for slimmers, including a medley of fresh fruits in individual foil parcels.

APPLE AND BANANA MERINGUE

Serves 4 / Preparation: 15 minutes / Cooking: 20 minutes

Fruit that may have passed its best in the fruit bowl gets a new lease on life in this simple sweet.

2 eating apples
2 bananas
45 ml (3 tbsp) lemon juice
25 g (1 oz) butter
2 eggs, separated
15 ml (1 tbsp) cornflour
150 ml (¼ pt) milk
15 ml (1 tbsp) granulated sugar
50 g (2 oz) caster sugar

1. Peel the apples, core and slice into rings. Place in a bowl. Peel and slice the bananas and add to the bowl with the lemon juice. Toss the fruit until coated.

2. Generously grease a straight-sided dish with the butter. Arrange the fruit on the base.

3. In a saucepan, mix the egg yolks and cornflour until smooth, then gradually stir in the milk and the granulated sugar. Place over the heat and cook, stirring constantly until thick and smooth. Pour over the fruit.

4. In a clean, dry bowl, whisk the egg whites until stiff. Fold in the caster sugar and spoon over the custard, making certain that it is completely covered.

5. Bake in a preheated over at 200°C (400°F), Gas Mark 6 for 20 minutes. Serve immediately.

MICROWAVE: the custard sauce may be made in a large jug in the microwave; it will take 3 minutes on HIGH power. Whisk after every 30 seconds. When thickened, pour the sauce over the fruit, top with meringue and bake in a conventional oven.

SPICY PEACHES

Serves 4 / Preparation and Cooking: 15 minutes plus chilling

This is a variation on a traditional brûlée, served in individual dishes and thus particularly suitable for eating while watching TV. Like all good productions, it provides a surprise in the opening moments; a pool of delectable spiced juice under the plain topping.

2 fresh peaches or 1 × 411 g (14½ oz) can peach slices in natural juice, drained
5 ml (1 tsp) cinnamon
90 ml (6 tbsp) demerara sugar
300 ml (10 fl oz) whipping cream

1. Skin and slice the peaches. Divide between 4 ramekin dishes.

2. Mix the cinnamon with 30 ml (2 tbsp) of the sugar in a small bowl. Sprinkle over the peaches and set aside.

3. In a bowl, whip the cream until it stands in soft peaks. Spread over the peaches to cover them completely.

4. Top with the remaining sugar, and place under a very hot grill until the sugar is caramelised.

5. Cool, then chill for 2–3 hours.

PEAR AND MINCEMEAT JALOUSIE

Serves 6 / Preparation: 15 minutes / Cooking: 20 minutes

Jalousies, puff pastry 'pies' with a distinctive slit lid, may be sweet or savoury. As you cut out the lid you may be reminded of paper lanterns you made as a child. These were cut in just the same way, but the edges of the paper were glued together, and a handle added.

225 g (8 oz) frozen puff pastry, thawed
125 g (4 oz) good-quality mincemeat
1 × 330 g (12 oz) can pears in natural juice, drained or 3 fresh pears,
peeled, cored and cut in half
125 g (4 oz) icing sugar
glacé cherries and angelica to decorate

1. Divide the pastry in half and roll out each half on a floured board to a rectangle 15 × 30 cm (6 × 12 in). Trim the edges.
2. Place one piece of pastry on a dampened baking sheet. Spread the mincemeat on the pastry, leaving a clear border all around.
3. Arrange the pear halves cut-side down on the top of the mincemeat.
4. Fold the second piece of pastry in half lengthways. With a sharp knife, make parallel cuts at 1 cm (½ in) intervals from the fold towards the doubled edge of the pastry, leaving a 1 cm (½ in) border uncut at the edge.
5. Unfold the pastry and lay it over the filling, damping the edges of the pastry so that top and bottom layers stick together. Scallop the edges of the jalousie and bake in a preheated oven at 200°C (400°F), Gas mark 6 for 20 minutes or until golden. Set aside to cool.

6. In a bowl, mix the icing sugar with a little water to make a thick glacé icing. Drizzle this over the jalousie and decorate with glacé cherries and angelica.

TIP: damping the baking sheet when cooking flaky or puff pastry will help the pastry to rise.

TOPSY-TURVY PLUM AND ALMOND PUDDING

**Serves 6 / Preparation: 15 minutes /
Cooking: 30 minutes plus standing**

As pretty as any picture on your TV screen, this is an appetizing answer to the problem of what to serve when plums are cheap and plentiful.

*25 g (1 oz) butter
15 ml (1 tbsp) golden syrup
225 g (8 oz) ripe plums, halved and stoned
25 g (1 oz) blanched almonds
125 g (4 oz) soft margarine
125 g (4 oz) soft light brown sugar
125 g (4 oz) fine self-raising wholemeal flour
2.5 ml (½ tsp) almond essence
2 eggs, beaten
30 ml (2 tbsp) milk*

1. Grease and base-line a 20 cm (8 in) cake tin or dish. Use the butter to grease both tin and lining paper thoroughly leaving the excess on the base.
2. Spoon the syrup into the tin and tilt to coat the base. Top with the plums, placing them cut side downwards, having first filled each stone cavity with an almond. Remember that the cooked pudding will be inverted to reveal your design.
3. Combine all the remaining ingredients in a mixing bowl and beat well for 2 minutes using a food mixer or hand-held electric beater. If beating by hand, increase the time to 3 minutes.
4. Spread the mixture over the plums and bake in a preheated oven at 190°C (375°F), Gas Mark 5 for 30 minutes or until the pudding is firm and golden on top.
5. Leave to stand for 5 minutes then turn out on to a plate and serve with custard.

MICROWAVE: this quantity cooks successfully in a cake dish. It will take 4½–5 minutes on HIGH power. Leave to stand for 5 minutes before turning out.

DRIED FRUIT COMPOTE

**Serves 4–6 / Preparation: 5 minutes plus soaking /
Cooking: 40 minutes**

High in fibre, vitamins and minerals, this is the perfect pud for anyone conscience-stricken about too much sitting on the sofa in front of the TV. It makes a warming winter dessert when served hot and any leftovers may be chilled in the refrigerator and eaten for breakfast. Choose a mixture of fruits for colour and flavour.

*450 g (1 lb) dried fruit (apricots, apples, prunes, figs)
50 g (2 oz) crystallised ginger, cut into small pieces
grated rind and juice of 1 orange
grated rind and juice of 1 lemon
75 g (3 oz) demerara sugar
30 ml (2 tbsp) dark rum (optional)*

1. Place the dried fruit in a heatproof bowl. Add the ginger, pour over boiling water to cover and leave to stand for 40 minutes.
2. Put the rind and juice of the fruit in a measuring jug. Stir in the sugar and make up to 600 ml (1 pt) with some of the soaking liquid from the dried fruit and ginger. Drain the dried fruit, discarding any remaining liquid.
3. Heat the fruit juice and sugar mixture in a large saucepan, stirring until all the sugar has dissolved. Stir in the fruit, cover and simmer gently for 30–40 minutes or until the fruit is tender.
4. Stir in the rum (if used) and serve hot or cold.

MICROWAVE: follow steps 1 and 2, then pour the fruit juice mixture into a large casserole. Heat on HIGH power for 3 minutes. Stir until the sugar has dissolved. Stir in the fruit, cover and cook on HIGH power for 12 minutes, then on MEDIUM power for 12 minutes or until the fruit is tender. Stir in the rum (if used) and serve as desired.

APPLE STRUDELS

Makes 8 / Preparation: 15 minutes / Cooking: 15 minutes

These are individual desserts which may be prepared in advance and stored in the freezer. You don't need to be an expert pastrycook as we have used filo pastry in ready-to-use sheets. This pastry is freely available in delicatessens or large supermarkets, but if you cannot find it, use thinly-rolled puff pastry instead. When using filo pastry, work swiftly as it dries out very quickly. If there is any delay at all, cover unused sheets with a clean damp tea towel.

25 g (1 oz) digestive biscuits
8 sheets of filo pastry
50 g (2 oz) butter, melted
675 g (1½ lb) cooking apples, peeled, cored and sliced
50 g (2 oz) raisins
30 ml (2 tbsp) caster sugar
cinnamon
icing sugar for dusting
butter for greasing

1. Have all the ingredients ready before you begin. Crush the digestive biscuits in a food processor or blender, or by placing between two sheets of greaseproof paper and crushing with a rolling pin.
2. Spread out all the sheets of pastry on a clean surface. Brush with melted butter, then fold each sheet in half to form a rough square. Brush again with butter.
3. Sprinkle a little crushed digestive biscuit on one corner of each square, then top with apple, raisins, sugar and a little cinnamon.
4. Roll up each pastry square from the corner, tucking in the edges as you go to form a neat parcel (see illustration below).
5. Place on a greased baking sheet, brush with more butter and bake in a preheated oven at 200°C (400°F), Gas Mark 6 for 10–15 minutes or until crisp and golden brown. Serve hot, sprinkled with icing sugar.

UPSIDE-DOWN APPLE TART

Serves 6 / Preparation: 15 minutes / Cooking: 20–25 minutes

This is our speedy version of the traditional *Tarte Tatin* which normally would use a rich, sweet pastry. Our recipe can literally be knocked together in minutes, but when served piping hot with fresh cream it tastes as though it came from the nearest French pâtisserie! Here, as elsewhere in the book, we have used frozen puff pastry for speed and convenience, but do use fresh if you have it.

50 g (2 oz) soft dark brown sugar
675 g (1½ lb) cooking apples, peeled, cored and thinly sliced
125 g (4 oz) frozen puff pastry, thawed
beaten egg or milk to glaze

1. Lightly grease a shallow 20 cm (8 in) sandwich cake tin. Sprinkle the sugar over the base and cover with the sliced apple.
2. On a floured board roll out the pastry to a round, roughly 20 cm (8 in) in diameter. Brush the sides of the tin with egg or milk, then cover the apples with the pastry lid. Press it down firmly, particularly at the edges, then trim.
3. Make a small hole in the centre of the pastry lid, brush with egg or milk and bake in a preheated oven at 200°C (400°F), Gas Mark 6 for 20–25 minutes or until golden brown. Invert on to a plate and serve.

APPLE SCONE CAKE

Serves 6 / Preparation: 15 minutes / Cooking: 35 minutes

Serve this substantial sweet with cream or custard and it will soon disappear. When time is short, use a packet of scone mix and a can of pie filling (try apricot or rhubarb for a change). The dessert does not use a whole can, so you could warm the remainder with a little water or fruit juice to serve as a sauce with the cake.

350 g (12 oz) self-raising flour
5 ml (1 tsp) baking powder
75 g (3 oz) caster sugar
75 g (3 oz) soft margarine
1 egg, beaten and made up to 200 ml (7 fl oz) with milk
350 g (12 oz) eating apples or
¾ × 396 g (14 oz) can apple pie filling
15–30 ml (1–2 tbsp) demerara sugar
butter for greasing

1. Sift the flour and baking powder into a mixing bowl and stir in the caster sugar.

2. Rub in the margarine until the mixture resembles breadcrumbs, then stir in the egg and milk mixture to make a soft scone dough. Do not overwork the dough.

3. Press two thirds of the dough on to the base of a greased 20 cm (8 in) round loose-bottomed cake tin.

4. Peel, core and slice the apples into a bowl. Sprinkle with 15 ml (1 tbsp) of the demerara sugar and spread over the dough. Alternatively, top the dough with the apple pie filling and omit the sugar.

5. Dot the remaining scone dough on the top, leaving the centre free. Sprinkle with the remaining sugar.

6. Bake in a preheated oven at 200°C (400°F), Gas Mark 6 for 35 minutes or until golden on top. Serve warm.

HOT FRUIT PARCELS

Serves 2 / Preparation: 10 minutes / Cooking: 10–15 minutes

This very simple and healthy recipe makes the most of your assets. It is particularly valuable as a means of making a little expensive fruit, such as out-of-season strawberries, go a long way. You need only add one or two per 175 g (6 oz) portion. Prepare these in advance and cook at the last moment. They will make lots of juice so serve each foil parcel in a bowl. Thick set Greek yogurt with clear honey makes an ideal accompaniment.

a selection of fresh fruit chosen from the following;
oranges, grapes, satsumas, mango, strawberries, raspberries, plums, bananas,
apples, peaches, apricots, pineapple

1. Prepare the fruit according to type. Spread two pieces of foil, each 23 cm (9 in) square, on a work surface. Divide the fruit between the foil squares, bring up the corners and twist to make two loose parcels.
2. Bake in a preheated oven at 180°C (350°F), Gas Mark 4 for 10–15 minutes and serve in the foil.

MICROWAVE: prepare the fruit but do not wrap it in foil. Divide it between individual bowls and heat on HIGH power for 1 minute each.

CARAMELISED BANANAS

Serves 4 / Preparation and Cooking: 10 minutes

These make a marvellous instant dessert to satisfy that craving for something sweet which usually arrives halfway through your favourite TV programme. Serve them with a dollop of ice cream and if you are feeling adventurous, flambé the bananas in brandy before serving! Drained canned peaches or apricots are equally delicious, so making this is simplicity itself if your store cupboard is well-stocked.

4 bananas
25 g (1 oz) butter
50 g (2 oz) demerara sugar
ice cream to serve

1. Slice the bananas in half lengthways. Melt the butter in a large frying pan, then stir in the sugar. Heat until the sugar dissolves.
2. Add the bananas to the pan and cook gently on one side until starting to soften, then turn over and cook the other side. Transfer carefully to individual bowls and serve immediately with ice cream.

> MICROWAVE: slice the bananas as above, then melt the butter in a large shallow dish on HIGH power for 1 minute. Stir in the sugar until dissolved, then turn the bananas over in the mixture. Cook on HIGH power for 3–4 minutes or until bananas are soft, turning carefully halfway through cooking.

FLAPJACK CRUMBLE

Serves 4 / Preparation: 15 minutes / Cooking: 35–40 minutes

This crumble has a particularly crunchy topping. It is easier to make than a traditional crumble, as there is no rubbing-in of the fat. For a slightly different flavour, try adding a little dried ginger to the fruit or topping if using pears or cinnamon if using apple.

1 kg (2¼ lb) fresh fruit (apples, pears, plums etc)
caster sugar
75 g (3 oz) margarine
50 g (2 oz) demerara sugar
75 g (3 oz) wholemeal flour
75 g (3 oz) rolled oats

1. Prepare the fruit according to type and place in a soufflé dish.
2. In a bowl beat the margarine with the sugar, then stir in the flour and oats. Sprinkle over the fruit and bake in a preheated over at 190°C (375°F), Gas Mark 5 for 35–40 minutes or until golden brown.

> MICROWAVE: as above but cook in the microwave on HIGH power for 12–14 minutes.

CHOCOLATE FUDGE PUDDING

Serves 6 / Preparation: 15 minutes / Cooking: 30 minutes

This is one of those magical puddings which seem fairly ordinary, but emerge from the oven as a light sponge with a really rich chocolate sauce. Serve it with plenty of single cream for your very own magic show.

125 g (4 oz) self-raising flour
25 g (1 oz) cocoa
50 g (2 oz) caster sugar
50 g (2 oz) blanched almonds, chopped (optional)
2.5 ml (½ tsp) vanilla essence
50 g (2 oz) butter, melted
150 ml (¼ pt) milk
butter for greasing

SAUCE
150 g (5 oz) soft light brown sugar
25 g (1 oz) cocoa
200 ml (7 fl oz) boiling water

1. Sift the flour and cocoa together into a mixing bowl. Add the sugar and almonds, then beat in the vanilla, butter and milk.
2. Pour into a greased 20 cm (8 in) soufflé dish.
3. In a small bowl, combine the sauce ingredients and mix well. Carefully pour over the cake mixture so that the sauce forms a layer on the top.
4. Bake in a preheated oven at 180°C (350°C), Gas Mark 4 for 30 minutes or until firm on top.

CHOCOLATE AND CHESTNUT POTS

Serves 6–8 / Preparation: 15 minutes plus chilling

Many of us (some more than others) crave chocolate in the evening – especially if watching something romantic. If you are a chocoholic, this recipe is a must! It is incredibly rich, so serve only in small portions – it keeps very well for several days in the refrigerator.

125 g (4 oz) unsalted butter, softened
125 g (4 oz) caster sugar
225 g (8 oz) plain chocolate
1 × 400 g (14 oz) can unsweetened chestnut purée
2.5 ml (½ tsp) vanilla essence
1 × 200 g (7 oz) can mandarin oranges, drained (optional)

1. In a mixing bowl, cream the butter and sugar together until light and fluffy.
2. Break the chocolate into squares and melt in a bowl set over a saucepan of boiling water.
3. Beat the melted chocolate into the butter mixture with the chestnut purée and vanilla essence. Spoon into individual ramekins or other small dishes, then chill for 1 hour in the refrigerator. Serve decorated with mandarin oranges, if liked.

MICROWAVE: follow step 1, then break the chocolate into squares and place in a bowl. Melt in the microwave on HIGH power for 2–4 minutes or until melted, stirring and checking regularly. Proceed from step 3.

LEMON SYLLABUB

Serves 4 / Preparation: 10 minutes plus chilling

Next time a food programme on TV leaves you hungry, but uncertain as to whether to have something to eat or drink, compromise by making this rich wine-based dessert. You can make Raspberry syllabub by adding 120 ml (8 tbsp) of Raspberry sauce (page 116) instead of the lemon juice, wine and sugar.

grated rind of 1 lemon
juice of ½ lemon
90 ml (6 tbsp) sweet white wine or cider
45 ml (3 tbsp) caster sugar
150 ml (5 fl oz) double cream

1. Combine the lemon rind, juice, wine and sugar in a mixing bowl and very gradually whisk in the cream. Continue to whisk until thick.
2. Pour into individual serving bowls and chill in the refrigerator before serving.

OLD-FASHIONED BREAD PUDDING

Serves 8 / Preparation: 10 minutes plus soaking / Cooking: 1 hour

We couldn't resist including this recipe; it's the sort of pudding that people buy from the bakers when they think no one is looking! We use a vegetarian suet that is higher in polyunsaturates than its beef equivalent but the choice is yours. Any leftovers will reheat very successfully.

225 g (8 oz) stale bread, crusts removed
175 g (6 oz) mixed dried fruit
75 g (3 oz) suet
75 g (3 oz) soft light brown sugar
2.5 ml (½ tsp) grated nutmeg
1 egg, beaten
milk (optional)
oil for greasing

1. Cut the bread into cubes and put it into a bowl. Add water to cover and leave to soak for 30 minutes.
2. Drain the bread, squeezing out as much water as possible. Return the bread to the bowl, add all the remaining ingredients and beat until well mixed. The mixture should drop easily from a spoon; if it is too thick add a little milk.
3. Pour into a greased 18 × 25 cm (7 × 10 in) baking dish or roasting tin. Level the surface and bake in a preheated oven at 190°C (375°F), Gas Mark 5 for 1 hour or until brown and firm. Serve warm.

DEB'S DELIGHT

Serves 4 / Preparation: 10 minutes plus standing and chilling

So called because it was an instant dessert often served by debutantes at dinner parties in the sixties. It is so simple to prepare but tastes like a ginger gâteau. Good to eat while watching a sixties classic!

1 × 200 g (7 oz) packet gingernut biscuits
45–60 ml (3–4 tbsp) medium sherry
150 ml (5 fl oz) double cream
grated chocolate to decorate

1. Carefully remove the biscuits from the wrappings, keeping them together. Place them, still in the log shape of the packet, on a serving plate.
2. Spoon the sherry over, making sure that each biscuit is well covered, and leave to stand until all the sherry has been absorbed.
3. In a bowl whip the cream until it stands in peaks, then spoon over the biscuit log, covering it completely. Chill in the refrigerator for 1 hour, then sprinkle with chocolate and serve.

FROZEN RASPBERRY MERINGUE ICE CREAM

Serves 4 / Preparation: 10 minutes plus freezing

This is a sinful sweet; very simple to make. If it has been frozen for more than a couple of hours transfer it to the refrigerator for 20 minutes before serving to soften.

300 ml (10 fl oz) double cream or whipping cream
125 g (4 oz) raspberries
30 ml (2 tbsp) orange liqueur or orange juice
125 g (4 oz) meringues

1. Whip the cream in a large bowl until it stands in soft peaks.
2. In a second bowl mash the raspberries with a fork until broken up. Stir in the orange liqueur or juice.
3. Break up but do not crush the meringues. Stir quickly and lightly into the cream with the raspberry mixture; do not aim to get it smooth or of an even colour. Pile into a pudding basin, cover and freeze for at least 2 hours or overnight.
4. Dip the basin into hot water for 30 seconds and turn out on a plate to serve.

FRESH ICE CREAM

Preparation: 15 minutes plus freezing

Nothing tastes better than home-made ice cream when it is well made. This is a foolproof recipe that does not call for an ice-cream maker, nor does it need to be removed from the freezer at regular intervals to be whisked. Do try it and keep a variety of flavours in store. As the eggs are not cooked, it is important that they are freshly purchased from a reliable supplier.

4 eggs (size 3), separated
125 g (4 oz) caster sugar
300 ml (10 fl oz) double cream
2.5 ml (½ tsp) vanilla essence

1. Place the egg yolks in a bowl and whisk until pale and thick. In a second, grease-free bowl whisk the whites until stiff, then gradually whisk in the sugar.
2. Use a third bowl for the cream, whipping it until it just holds its shape. Whisk in the vanilla essence.

3. Carefully fold all the ingredients together. Pour into a container, cover and freeze. Remove from the freezer 5–10 minutes before serving to allow the ice cream to soften and any flavouring to develop.

Variations

- Fold in a little Chocolate sauce (see page 116)
- Fold in a little Butterscotch sauce (see below)
- Fold in a little Raspberry sauce (see page 116)
- Add chopped pistachio nuts
- Add chocolate chips
- Add a little rum and some raisins

> TIP: Fresh ice cream can form the basis of every child's favourite dessert – the Knickerbocker glory! To make, take ½ X 142 g (5 oz) packet raspberry jelly and make up following the instructions on the packet but using only 300 ml (½ pt) water. Divide between 4 sundae or tall glasses. Leave to set. When the jelly is firm, place a few peach slices on top, then add a few slices of banana and a scoop of ice cream to each glass. Pour over a little Raspberry sauce (page 116). Repeat the layers until all the fruit is used up. Decorate each sundae with a swirl of whipped cream, sprinkle with chopped nuts and top with a glacé cherry. Serve immediately.

BUTTERSCOTCH SAUCE

Serves 4–6 / Preparation and Cooking: 10 minutes

Serve this sauce with ice cream or freshly sliced oranges. It reheats very successfully.

50 g (2 oz) butter
50 g (2 oz) golden syrup
125 g (4 oz) demerara sugar

1. Combine all the ingredients in a heavy-bottomed saucepan and melt over gentle heat. Bring to the boil and boil until golden brown.

> MICROWAVE: combine all the ingredients in a bowl and heat on HIGH power for 5 minutes. Stir until all the sugar has dissolved then return to the oven and cook on HIGH power for 5–7 minutes or until golden brown.

CHOCOLATE SAUCE

Makes 150 ml (¼ pt) / Preparation and Cooking: 10 minutes

This sauce may be made in advance and stored in a bowl in the refrigerator. To reheat either set the bowl over a saucepan of hot water or heat in the microwave. It is delicious with ice cream, sponge pudding or profiteroles.

125 g (4 oz) plain chocolate
15 g (½ oz) butter
30 ml (2 tbsp) golden syrup
30 ml (2 tbsp) water

1. Break the chocolate into squares. Place in a bowl set over a saucepan of gently simmering water. Heat until melted, stirring occasionally.
2. Beat in the remaining ingredients and serve.

MICROWAVE: place the chocolate squares in a bowl with all the remaining ingredients. Heat on HIGH power for 2–4 minutes or until the chocolate has melted and the sauce is smooth, stirring and checking frequently.

RASPBERRY SAUCE

Makes 300 ml (½ pt) / Preparation: 10 minutes

This sauce is invaluable for dressing-up desserts and other dishes. Use it over plain ice cream or with brandy snaps filled with cream. Meringues filled with cream and laid on a pool of this sauce look wonderful and canned peaches topped with this become peach melba, so it is worth making in bulk when raspberries are in season, and freezing in small amounts.

225 g (8 oz) raspberries
juice of ½ orange
50 g (2 oz) icing sugar or to taste

1. Combine all the ingredients in the bowl of a blender or food processor. Blend for 20 seconds and then push through a fine sieve into a bowl or jug. Alternatively, cream the orange juice and sugar in a bowl. Mash the raspberries and beat them into the mixture, then sieve.

TIP: when sieving vegetable or fruit purées, use a soup ladle to press the mixture though the sieve; the greater surface area gives speedier results.

QUICK CONFECTIONERS' CUSTARD

Serves 4 / Preparation and Cooking: 10 minutes

In less time than it takes to make an instant custard from powder, this freshly made custard can be prepared. Simply mix all the ingredients in a saucepan and whisk over gentle heat until thickened. Use the custard hot as a pouring sauce or cold in pastry cases as a base for a fresh fruit topping.

15 ml (1 tbsp) cornflour
300 ml (½ pt) milk
25 g (1 oz) caster sugar
1 egg
2.5 ml (½ tsp) vanilla essence

1. In a cup, mix the cornflour to a paste with a little of the milk.
2. Pour the remaining milk into a saucepan. Add the sugar, egg and cornflour paste and whisk over gentle heat until thick. Remove from the heat and whisk in the vanilla essence.
3. If the custard is to be served hot you may wish to add a little more milk. If served cold, cover the surface of the custard with a dampened piece of greaseproof paper and stand the saucepan in a bowl of cold water.

MICROWAVE: follow step 1, but combine the ingredients in a bowl or wide-mouthed jug. Cook on HIGH power for 3–4 minutes, whisking regularly. Whisk in the vanilla essence. Proceed as in step 3.

TIP: a quick vanilla slice may be made with 225 g (8 oz) puff pastry. Roll it to an oblong, trim the edges and bake until well risen. Allow to cool before splitting in half and filling with confectioners' custard. Top with glacé icing, made by mixing sifted icing sugar to a thin cream with cold water.

GINGERBREAD MEN

Makes 18 / Preparation: 15 minutes / Cooking: 10–15 minutes

While their programmes are on, children enjoy something to munch. These tasty biscuits are perfect. We have cut down the quantity of ginger; in our experience, children don't like anything too spicy. If you are feeling creative decorate the biscuits or, better still, leave this to the children.

350 g (12 oz) plain flour
5 ml (1 tsp) bicarbonate of soda
5 ml (1 tsp) ground ginger
125 g (4 oz) butter
125 g (4 oz) soft light brown sugar
grated rind of 1 lemon
1 egg, beaten
60 ml (4 tbsp) golden syrup, slightly warmed
oil for greasing

1. Sift the flour, bicarbonate of soda and ginger into a mixing bowl and rub in the butter until the mixture resembles breadcrumbs.
2. Stir in the sugar and lemon rind, then add the egg and syrup. Stir well, then knead gently until smooth.
3. On a floured board, roll out the biscuit dough. Using a gingerbread cutter or a cardboard template, cut out about 18 gingerbread men, re-rolling and re-cutting any trimmings.
4. Place the shapes on greased baking sheets and bake in a preheated oven at 190°C (375°F), Gas Mark 5 for 10–15 minutes or until golden. Transfer to a wire rack to cool.

MAGICAL MUESLI COOKIES

Makes 30 / Preparation: 10 minutes / Cooking: 15 minutes

The magical thing about these light crumbly biscuits is how fast they disappear. Fit a false bottom to the biscuit tin if you want to save some for late night nibbling. They will keep for up to a week.

125 g (4 oz) white vegetable fat
125 g (4 oz) soft light brown sugar
1 egg, beaten
125 g (4 oz) self-raising flour
150 g (5 oz) muesli
oil for greasing

1. Cream the fat with the sugar in a mixing bowl until light and fluffy.
2. Beat in the egg, then stir in the remaining ingredients.
3. Put teaspoons of the mixture on to greased baking sheets, allowing plenty of space for spreading.
4. Bake in a preheated oven at 190°C (375°F), Gas Mark 5 for 15 minutes or until pale gold. Transfer to a wire rack to cool.

CHOCOLATE FRUIT AND NUT BARS

Makes about 15 / Preparation and Cooking: 15 minutes plus chilling

Children love to make these no-bake biscuits and need supervision only when melting the chocolate mixture.

175 g (6 oz) digestive biscuits, crushed (see Apple strudels, page 105)
50 g (2 oz) chopped mixed nuts or chopped glacé cherries
50 g (2 oz) raisins
50 g (2 oz) plain chocolate
30 ml (2 tbsp) golden syrup
50 g (2 oz) butter
oil for greasing

1. Combine the biscuit crumbs, nuts or cherries and raisins in a bowl.
2. Break the chocolate into squares; place with syrup and butter in a bowl over a pan of gently simmering water. Allow to melt, stirring occasionally.
3. Pour the chocolate mixture over the biscuits, nuts and raisins and stir until well coated.
4. Press into a greased and base-lined 18 cm (7 in) square tin, then chill until set. Cut into bars to serve.

MICROWAVE: follow step 1, then place the chocolate squares in a bowl with the golden syrup and butter. Heat on HIGH power for 2-3 minutes or until melted, stirring frequently. Proceed as in steps 3 and 4.

CHOCOLATE AND ORANGE COOKIES

**Makes about 30 / Preparation: 15 minutes plus chilling /
Cooking: 8–10 minutes**

Whether Saturday afternoons spell sport or sentimental old films, these scrumptuous biscuits will add a certain something to the occasion. Freeze the dough in a roll wrapped in bakewell paper. When guests call unexpectedly, cut the frozen dough in slices, transfer to baking sheets and bake. In the time it takes to make a pot of tea and set a tray, you'll be able to produce a batch of home-made biscuits.

150 g (5 oz) margarine
175 g (6 oz) caster sugar
1 egg, beaten
grated rind of 1 orange
25 g (1 oz) chocolate chips
275 g (10 oz) self-raising flour

1. Cream the margarine and caster sugar in a mixing bowl, then beat in the egg and orange rind.
2. Fold in the chocolate chips and flour, then knead together lightly and form into two sausage shapes, approximately 4 cm (1½ in) in diameter.
3. Wrap each roll in bakewell paper and chill in the refrigerator for 2 hours or overwrap in a freezer bag and freeze.
4. When required, cut the biscuit rolls into thin slices and bake on a greased baking sheet in a preheated oven at 200°C (400°F), Gas Mark 6 for 8–10 minutes.

ICED LEMON SPICE BISCUITS

Makes 16 / Preparation: 15 minutes / Cooking: 30 minutes

Simply delicious – that describes these crisp shortbread biscuits with a sharp lemon icing. We often double or treble the quantities and freeze the surplus in a plastic bag at the end of step 2, then, when we want biscuits in a hurry all we have to do is shake the mixture into the tins and bake.

125 g (4 oz) butter
75 g (3 oz) caster sugar
75 g (3 oz) plain flour
75 g (3 oz) wholemeal flour
2.5 ml (½ tsp) mixed spice
grated rind of 1 lemon
oil for greasing

DECORATION (OPTIONAL)
75 g (3 oz) icing sugar
lemon juice

1. Cream the butter with the sugar until soft and creamy; a mixer is ideal for this.
2. Sift the plain and wholemeal flours and spice into a bowl, adding the residue in the sieve. Add to the creamed butter, with the lemon rind. Stir well. The mixture does not need to form a ball.
3. Sprinkle the mixture into two lightly greased 18 cm (7 in) sandwich cake tins and press down firmly.
4. Bake in a preheated oven at 160°C (325°F), Gas Mark 3 for 30 minutes.
5. Cut into triangles while still warm but leave in the tins.
6. If liked, make a smooth glacé icing by mixing the icing sugar with a little lemon juice. Drizzle the icing over the biscuits while they are still warm.
7. When the biscuits are cool and any icing has set, remove from the tins.

THE
LATE NIGHT MOVIE

A selection of drinks to stimulate or soothe, depending on your plans for the evening. A quick Martini (shaken not stirred) will see you through the James Bond movie and a Malted sleepmaker will calm your nerves after the late night spine-chiller. If your throat is sore after cheering your favourite team in the cup final, a St Clement's cup will soothe, and if your team lost a Liqueur coffee may dull your disappointment. All the hot drinks can be made in the microwave (to make use a large measuring jug and check regularly). So whatever your pleasure, you'll be tasting it soon.

FLOATING CLOUDS

Serves 4 / Preparation and Cooking: 5 minutes

This is without doubt the best hot chocolate we have ever tasted! Sipped through a layer of melting marshallows it's the perfect way to unwind.

600 ml (1 pt) milk
50 g (2 oz) plain chocolate
15 ml (1 tbsp) sugar
4 marshmallows

1. Pour the milk into a saucepan. Break the chocolate into squares and add to the milk with the sugar.
2. Heat gently, stirring occasionally until all the chocolate has dissolved and the milk is hot. Pour into cups and float a marshmallow on top to serve.

MOCHA

Serves 2 / Preparation and Cooking: 5 minutes

It is said that chocolate is as good as a hug; personally we would rather have both! So cuddle up on the sofa and watch the late night movie while you sip this lovely warming drink. The cream in an aerosol is ideal for the topping.

300 ml (½ pt) milk
150 ml (¼ pt) water
10 ml (2 tsp) instant coffee
30 ml (2 tbsp) instant hot chocolate
whipped cream
a little grated chocolate or hot chocolate powder

1. Heat the milk, water and coffee in a saucepan until almost boiling.
2. Whisk in the chocolate powder and pour into 2 mugs or heatproof glasses.
3. Spoon a little whipped cream on top of each and sprinkle with grated chocolate or hot chocolate powder. Drink immediately.

HOT MALTED SLEEPMAKER

Serves 2 / Preparation and Cooking: 5 minutes

Round off the evening with this comforter, and ensure a good night's sleep despite watching the late-night horror film.

5 ml (1 tsp) Ovaltine
5 ml (1 tsp) drinking chocolate
350 ml (12 fl oz) milk
15 ml (1 tbsp) brandy
10 ml (2 tsp) grated chocolate

1. Combine the Ovaltine and drinking chocolate in a saucepan and gradually whisk in the milk. Heat until almost boiling. Remove from heat and stir in brandy. Pour into mugs and serve sprinkled with grated chocolate.

ST CLEMENT'S CUP

Serves 2 / Preparation and Cooking: 10 minutes

When you feel a cold coming on indulge yourself with this warming non-alcoholic fruit cup. Drink it just before bedtime and enjoy the soothing effect and the thought of all those freshly-squeezed vitamins!

250 ml (8 fl oz) water
2 strips orange rind, without the pith
2 strips lemon rind, without the pith
juice of 1 orange and 1 lemon
10 ml (2 tsp) honey

1. Combine all the ingredients in a small saucepan and heat until almost boiling. Pour into cups or heatproof glasses and serve.

LIQUEUR COFFEE

Serves 2 / Preparation: 5 minutes

Half the fun of this popular drink is experimenting to find the liqueur or spirit whose flavour you like best. It's highly alcoholic though, so save it for home consumption. Don't overdo it – you need a steady hand to pour the cream. Adding plenty of sugar will help the cream to float.

300 ml (½ pt) good hot black coffee
90 ml (3 fl oz) whiskey, rum, brandy, vodka or liqueur of own choice
15 ml (1 tbsp) sugar
60 ml (4 tbsp) single cream or whipped double cream

1. Pour the coffee and spirit or liqueur into cups or heatproof glasses and sweeten to taste.
2. Pour single cream into each cup or glass over the back of a tablespoon whose tip rests on the surface of the coffee. The cream should float on the surface. If using whipped cream, simply spoon it on top. Serve immediately.

MULLED WINE

**Makes 1 litre (1¾ pt) / Preparation: 5 minutes plus standing /
Cooking: 5 minutes**

Come home on a chilly winter's night to a glass of mulled wine and the
promise of a good evening's viewing.

300 ml (½ pt) unsweetened orange juice
50 g (2 oz) soft light brown sugar
1.25 ml (¼ tsp) ground cloves
2.5 ml (½ tsp) cinnamon
1 orange, 1 lemon sliced
1 standard bottle red wine
175 ml (6 fl oz) dry Martini
30 ml (2 tbsp) gin

1. Combine the orange juice, sugar and spices in a large saucepan. Bring to
the boil, stirring until the sugar has dissolved.
2. Remove from the heat and add the orange and lemon slices. Leave to
stand for 10 minutes, then stir in the wine, Martini and gin and heat
through. Do not boil. If wished, strain and serve with fresh sliced fruit.

YO HO HO PUNCH

Makes 6 glasses / Preparation: 5 minutes plus cooling

A delicious thirst quencher which can easily be made in larger quantities.

400 ml (14 fl oz) medium dry white wine
30 ml (2 tbsp) rum
½ × 178 ml (6¼ fl oz) can frozen concentrated orange juice
1 orange, thinly sliced
300 ml (½ pt) lemonade

1. Combine the wine, rum, undiluted orange juice and sliced orange in a
large jug. Mix well, then leave to stand in the refrigerator for 1 hour.
2. Stir in the lemonade, with ice to chill, and serve.

MARTINI

Serves 2 / Preparation: 5 minutes

Next time there's a James Bond movie on TV you can join in as well as watch. His instructions are always to shake not stir so make sure you do the same!

1 measure gin
2 measures dry vermouth
6 ice cubes
lemon peel twists

1. Combine the gin, vermouth and ice in a cocktail shaker and shake well until very cold.
2. Pour into 2 glasses and garnish each with a lemon peel twist.

INDEX